DO YOU KNOW . . .

- The mortality rate for anorexia is higher than for any other psychiatric disorder.
- A tendency for eating disorders can be inherited, and you can evaluate your family to see if you or your child is at risk.
- Most, if not all, eating disorders begin wth a single diet.
- There are concrete steps parents can take to prevent eating disorders . . . and they can start as early as infancy.
- Pinpointing triggers of stress, a major component in eating disorders, is essential . . . and there's an easy way to do it.

FIND OUT MORE IN . . .

If You Think You Have
AN EATING DISORDER

Look for these other Dell Guides for Mental Health:

If You Think You Have Depression
If You Think You Have Panic Disorder
If You Think You Have Seasonal Affective Disorder
If You Think You Have a Sleep Disorder

A DELL MENTAL HEALTH GUIDE

If You Think You Have an

EATING DISORDER

John W. Barnhill, M.D.,
and
Nadine Taylor, M.S., R.D.

A DELL BOOK

Published by
Dell Publishing
a division of
Bantam Doubleday Dell Publishing Group, Inc.
1540 Broadway
New York, New York 10036

ISBN: 0-440-22538-8

Printed in the United States of America

Published simultaneously in Canada

May 1998

10 9 8 7 6 5 4 3 2 1

OPM

Note to Reader

*For every young girl who doesn't realize that
she's perfect just the way she is . . .*

Contents

Foreword

For most of history, our ancestors struggled mightily to fend off starvation. For the greater part of this century, this struggle has been over for middle-class Westerners. The farmers have won. We have more food than we need.

Despite the excess, however, food-related problems persist. We have written this book to help those of you who are struggling with an eating disorder, a problem that echoes the biblical adage that water is everywhere but there's not a drop to drink. Whether it is hunger related to anorexia, or hunger that is part of a binge-and-purge cycle, we have a big starvation problem in today's society.

Although the book is written so that you can begin by reading whatever most interests you, we do suggest that you first try to understand these disorders before you launch into some sort of treatment. While there is a variety of problems related to eating, we are going to focus on anorexia and bulimia.

Anorexia nervosa is an illness in which someone is too thin and is overly fearful of getting fat. In some way, bulimia nervosa is similar to anorexia. For example, both disorders are characterized by dieting and hunger. People with bulimia do not maintain their diets with the same rigor, however, as anorexics. Instead, after some period of starvation, which can be hours or days, the bulimic loses control of her hunger and eats a huge amount of food. These food binges are usually accompanied by great remorse and shame. The bulimic will then compensate by doing something to get rid of the consumed calories. To purge herself, for example, she might make herself vomit or take laxatives or overexercise or starve herself. Bulimia nervosa can be seen as a cycle of hunger-binge-purge-hunger. Like the anorexic, the bulimic can become totally preoccupied with her diet and body shape. Unlike the anorexic, however, the bulimic is of average or above average weight. If someone engages in bulimic behavior and is too thin, she is better characterized as an anorexic who binges and purges. We will elaborate on these definitions in the first chapter.

The vast majority of people with eating disorders are intelligent and knowledgeable people, and many are highly successful in school and work. How do bright people develop such an unhappy relationship with food? What is it that makes them anorexic and bulimic? Are there common patterns in the families or childhoods of people who go on to develop eating disorders? No one has the complete answers to such questions, but quite a lot is known. For example, we know that anorexia develops in people who tend to be perfectionistic, controlling, and unhappy, and that bulimia develops within people who tend toward self-criticism and impulsivity. But having these—and other—personality characteristics is not enough. Anorexia and bulimia don't develop in cultures where there is not a lot of food and where there is not an idealization of a particular type of body. During recent decades in the West, the ideal has been a thin, athletic body. The image of this ideal is everywhere. We see it in magazines and on television, and we hear it every day at school and at work. Much of this propaganda is aimed at teenage girls, who are expected to fulfill an idealized fantasy while also developing themselves into independent young women. These two opposing goals create a conflict that often leads to a lot of unhappiness and frustration. Furthermore, even with rigorous effort, few are capable of reaching this ideal, and even those who do—like models and actresses—are often beset by severe eating disorders. Yet, societal pressures are not enough to cause anorexia or bulimia. While most young women emerge from puberty with some food-related issues, only a small percent develop an eating disorder.

In addition to having similar personalities and cultural backgrounds, young women with eating disorders tend to have grown up within similar kinds of families. In talking about typical family structures, we are treading on thin ice. It is painful enough to have your loved one go through the trauma of an eating disorder without experts blaming you for it. We want to make it clear that although we believe that certain family problems can initiate and intensify an eating disorder, we also believe that there is rarely one culprit to blame for the problem. Instead, we see the family as moving around in a complex dance of which they are only partially aware. For example, if a girl grows up in a household where she is her mother's best friend, and where there is a lot of hidden anger between the parents, the girl might learn instinctively that she has to give up her independence in order to save her mother and save the marriage. The girl might become, for example, a model child, with a very neat room and a very quick smile. Not only might this help out her parents' relationship, it could provide her with a feeling of self-worth and a feeling of superiority over her neighbors and siblings. In a lot of ways, this development is a reasonable compromise to a difficult situation. At the same time, the effort doesn't really match her own interests, and the girl might not learn to be her own person and experience her own feelings. With puberty and its demand for greater independence and maturity, the girl might begin to feel an enormous sense of inadequacy. How is she going to stay perfect? How is she going to match up to the images on television? How can she avoid some of the difficulties of growing up, like sex and independence? How is she going to gain control over the situation? Given the right circumstances, the budding woman might focus on something she does control: food. Anorexia or bulimia might develop.

In the book, we explore typical family scenarios to help you begin to think about ways you might unintentionally be hurting yourself or the people you love. How do we know if we're too close to our child or our mother? How do we know if we're adequately independent? How do we know if we are unconsciously sabotaging the recovery of our loved one? These aren't easy concepts to understand, but we will explore them and suggest ways for you to proceed.

For most people with eating disorders, a consultation with experts will be necessary. Therapists, physicians, and nutritionists may all be of use, and we will discuss how you can find such people. For a variety of reasons, getting started can be the slowest part of the whole process. If you think you might have an eating disorder, now might be the time to find a quiet spot and read through the book and see what seems to apply to your situation. Let your curiosity take over. This can be a great opportunity to look at yourself with gentle honesty.

One of the interesting aspects of writing this book was that we each work in different fields and have somewhat different perspectives on eating disorders. Throughout the book we tried to include what we each believe, as well as the beliefs of the most current theoreticians and therapists, and we tried to make sure our discussion was coherent. When there were differences in philosophy, we made a clear decision to favor being comprehensive. For example, we end the book with a set of daily affirmations that you can use. For some people, affirmations work. For others, affirmations may seem like a waste of time. In this case, and others, we offer you the choice of using or not using the material.

Much of the book comes down to this issue: choice.

People with eating disorders are usually stuck in an unhappy rut; they see no way out. If they change their eating habits, they believe they'll get fat. If they change the way that they interact with the world, they'll lose the scrap of control that they've achieved. If they become more genuinely assertive, they'll lose their families. The details differ, but Hilde Bruch called their predicament "a golden cage." It is our goal to help you free yourself from the invisible ties that bind and to act and feel more flexible within your world. At the moment, recovery from an eating disorder may seem like a huge task, but it can also be part of a process of self-discovery that can allow you to be happier and freer than you've ever known. Good luck with your journey, and, in the meantime, try to be kind to yourself.

Chapter One

FROM DIET TO DESTRUCTION: THREE KINDS OF EATING DISORDERS

I'd rather be dead than fat.
　　　　　　　　　—Jenny, sixteen-year-old anorexic

In 1983, at the age of thirty-two, Karen Carpenter died from complications of anorexia nervosa. She had struggled with the disease for seven years. Her journey from "cutting back a little to take off a few pounds" to death by starvation was fraught with desperation, agony, and despair. But in the end, nothing could stem the tide of her Herculean willpower, which kept her firmly on the path to self-destruction until it finally "won" the ultimate battle. At times, Karen took ninety to a hundred laxative tablets a day in an effort to "get rid of" any food she had eaten, coupled with ten times the typical dosage of thyroid-stimulating medication to speed up her metabolism and burn calories. Her family tried everything they could think of: heart-to-heart talks, screaming, and pleading, but in the end they could only stand by, helplessly watching as she tumbled headlong into the abyss.

At the time of Karen's death, little was known about the causes, treatment, and prevention of eating disorders. Since then, our ability to treat these diseases through psychological intervention, medication, nutrition education, and other means has improved, but we still don't have the complete answer to one vital question: What makes a person insist on starving herself, even to the point of death? We do know that there may be certain physical causes, relationship problems within the family, an unnatural desire for "perfection," an unbridled desire for control, an inability to deal with stress, or some combination of these factors. But we're still unsure why one person can manage to diet with no ill effects while another goes off the deep end. One thing is certain: Most eating disorders begin with restrictive or "fad" dieting. But the exact set of circumstances that produce the full-blown illness is unique to each individual.

In this book we'll look at the "thinness mania" that has engulfed our society, and explore the reasons that diets are downright dangerous. We'll pinpoint who among us is most likely to develop an eating disorder. We'll examine both the physical and the psychological causes of these diseases and investigate the current therapies. We'll detail coping strategies for the families and friends of eating disorder victims, who struggle with their own problems as well as those of their loved ones. In the chapter on prevention, we'll show you how to keep your children from falling into the eating disorder trap. And finally, we'll show you how and where to get help if you or a loved one should need it. But first, let's define the problem.

What are eating disorders?

A lot of people have eating habits that could be considered "strange." Some are extremely "picky" eaters, consuming only a few kinds of foods. Some are ritualistic about their food, eating certain foods only at certain times or in certain combinations (e.g., no fruit after 3:00 P.M. or no mixing of protein and carbohydrate). Others slather practically everything they eat with mustard. Are any of these habits symptoms of an eating disorder? By themselves, no. To put it concisely, if your eating habits are hurtful to you, then you have an eating disorder. It's as simple as that.

But if you use that definition, *everybody* would have an eating disorder . . .

Not really, although it might seem that way. We have an excess of food in the West, and for most of us, adequate calories have become a given. At the same time, food, hunger, and body shape have taken on enormous symbolic, personal, and interpersonal importance for most of us. So eating *issues* have become pervasive in our culture. Eating *disorders*, on the other hand, are less common. Obviously, there is a gray area between people with eating issues and those with eating disorders. For the purposes of this book, we will use the eating disorder definitions found in the *DSM-IV*.

What is the DSM-IV?

The *DSM-IV* (short for *Diagnostic and Statistical Manual of Mental Disorders*, fourth edition) is the official reference book of psychiatric diagnoses. Yes, eating disorders are officially classified as mental disorders rather than physical ones even though the victim's physical state is very much influenced by the condition. But this wasn't always the case. Before 1980 the *DSM* buried anorexia in a section titled "Special Symptoms: Feeding Disturbance," while bulimia wasn't included at all because so little was known about it. Only fairly recently did the *DSM* begin to designate a special section just for eating disorders. Today three major kinds of eating disorders are recognized.

What are the three kinds of eating disorders?

The *DSM-IV* recognizes and describes diagnostic criteria for:

anorexia nervosa—characterized by an individual who refuses to maintain a minimally normal body weight;

bulimia nervosa—characterized by an individual who engages in repeated incidences of binge eating, then compensates for the excess calories by inducing vomiting; misusing laxatives, diuretics, or other medications; and fasting or exercising excessively;

eating disorders not otherwise specified—a sort of "catch-all" category for disturbances in eating behavior that don't fit neatly into either of the first two categories. Binge Eating Disorder, which involves the binge eating seen in bulimia *without* the compensatory vomiting, laxative abuse, etc., falls into this classification.

What is anorexia nervosa?

A person with anorexia nervosa consciously maintains her weight at a level lower than the low end of the normal weight spectrum for her height (usually less than 85 percent of the "expected weight"). It's not always easy to distinguish anorexia from thinness since many people are thin because of genetic reasons or simply because they exercise a lot or don't eat much. The primary difference between thinness and anorexia is the way the anorexic experiences her body shape and size. She[1] is terrified of becoming fat or gaining weight, has stopped menstruating because her body fat has dropped below a certain level, and has a distorted sense of her body size and shape, feeling "fat" even when she isn't.

Coming from the Greek words *an* ("lack of"), *orexis* ("appetite"), and *nervosa* ("mental disorder"), *anorexia nervosa* literally means "lack of appetite due to a mental disorder." But that's not a totally accurate description of the illness. Most anorexics actually have a tremendous desire to eat, spending nearly every waking moment thinking about food. Up to 50 percent of anorexics eventually give in to their appetites, eating enormous amounts of food in a short period of time (bingeing). But given their overwhelming fear of weight gain, anorexics who binge usually find a way to get rid of the calories. They purge (by inducing vomiting or using laxatives, diuretics, or enemas to remove calories, fat, or pounds from the body), fast, or exercise obsessively.

In general, though, the anorexic is able to reach her very low body weight by one method—drastically reducing her intake of food. She is driven to do this by her all-consuming fear of becoming fat, her self-esteem having become entirely dependent upon her ability to get thin or fit into smaller-and-smaller-sized clothes. Soon thinness becomes an obsession; she might compulsively weigh herself several times a day, measure certain areas of her body over and over, and constantly check her reflection in the mirror to see if her bones are protruding far enough. For her, weight loss is equated with achievement and self-control, weight gain with failure and shame. Although serious medical complications accompany this illness, the anorexic will deny that anything is wrong, insisting that she feels "fine."

What are the diagnostic criteria for anorexia nervosa?

A victim of anorexia will exhibit most (if not all) of these symptoms:

- She refuses to maintain a normal body weight for her age and height.
- She weighs less than 85 percent of what is expected for her age and height.
- She misses at least three consecutive menstrual cycles (or, if prepubertal when weight loss begins, she doesn't start her menstrual cycle at an appropriate age).
- She has an intense fear of gaining weight or "getting fat," even though she is underweight. That fear doesn't subside, even as her weight loss progresses.
- She denies the seriousness of her low body weight.

- She feels "fat" even though she is very thin.
- She places undue importance on her body weight and/or shape in her self-evaluation.
- She has no known physical condition that would account for her low weight.

In addition, the anorexic is often subject to many of the mental and emotional characteristics seen in starvation: she's depressed, irritable, and withdrawn. She has trouble sleeping and shows a lack of interest in sex. Obsessed with food, she thinks about it constantly, carefully planning what she will allow herself to eat, poring over recipes and menus, and cooking for and feeding others. She even dreams about food. She may develop strange ritualistic behaviors such as cutting her food into tiny pieces, counting the number of times she chews each bite, or squirreling food away into secret hiding places (although she never eats it). She may also refuse to eat in front of anyone, feeling that it's "too private an act."

Is there more than one kind of anorexic?

Although all anorexics exhibit most of these characteristics, they can be divided into two subgroups according to the *way* they eat. They are either the *restricting type* or the *binge eating/purging type*. The *restricting type* simply cuts back on her food intake (often, but not always, to the point of starvation) to reach her goal of unnatural thinness.

Gelsey Kirkland, who danced brilliantly for American Ballet Theatre in the 1970s, is a good example of the restricting type of anorexic. She devised a special "diet" for herself while recuperating from a shattered ankle. Afraid that she would gain weight because she was laid up on the couch and couldn't exercise, Gelsey's goal was to stay at ninety pounds. In her book, *Danc-*

ing on My Grave, she describes her typical day's food intake while on the "diet":

> In the morning I sliced one green apple into four pieces. Each piece constituted one "meal," with a tablespoon of cottage cheese for dessert. I ate four "meals" a day. . . . I was proud of myself for keeping my physical instrument tuned to perfection.[2]

The other type of anorexic, the *binge eating/purging type*, may eat normal to large quantities of food regularly while purging, fasting, or engaging in excessive exercise to keep her weight at an extremely low level. Or she may purge regularly even if she hasn't binged. Karen Carpenter fell into this category. Although she was not a binger (indeed, most days she ate next to nothing), she was definitely a purger. In fact, Karen's chronic use of up to a hundred laxative pills per day eventually did so much damage to her digestive system that she had to undergo intravenous refeeding.[3] Her body simply couldn't handle normal amounts of food anymore.

What are the physical consequences of anorexia?

As far as the body is concerned, anorexia and starvation are the same thing, and the consequences of the two are identical. The most shockingly obvious characteristic is extreme physical emaciation. The bones protrude from the flesh, the arms and legs are like matchsticks, the face is gaunt, and the eyes are sunken in their hollows. One mother described her anorexic daughter this way:

> I knew she was very thin, but I really wasn't aware of how bad it had gotten, because she always wore big, baggy clothes that hid her shape. Then one day we went to the doctor and I stayed in the room while he examined her. What I saw absolutely stunned me. You could

count every single rib and every vertebra in her back
from across the room. Her pelvic bones stuck out so far
she looked deformed. There wasn't the least bit of curve
or softness to any part of her body, including her der-
riere. She looked like a walking skeleton.

During the course of her illness, an anorexic will
typically lose anywhere from 15 to 50 percent of her
original body weight, meaning that a 120-pound young
woman could end up weighing a heart-stopping 60
pounds! Over time, as her body continues to be de-
prived of an adequate energy supply, it will use up its
fat stores and slow vital functions to conserve energy.
The basal metabolic rate (the "speed" at which the
body burns calories just to stay alive) will drop. The
heart will beat slower, and blood pressure will fall.
With her circulation slow and poor, an anorexic may
feel dizzy, suffer from fainting spells, and always feel
cold, bundling up in heavy clothing even during warm
weather. In response to this chronic chilliness, her body
may cover itself with a layer of fine hair (called lanugo
hair). If her low blood pressure causes a prolonged
reduction of blood supply to the kidneys, they may mal-
function or fail. Some anorexics wind up on kidney di-
alysis for life as a direct result of their eating disorders.
When body fat drops to a certain level, estrogen production lessens, causing menstruation to cease. It's as if
the body realizes that there isn't enough food to support
a pregnancy, so it dispenses with menstruation, consid-
ering it an optional function. Lack of estrogen can also
cause osteoporosis, the "hollowing" of the bones to the
point where they begin to look like honeycomb. This is
made worse by the anorexic's lack of dietary calcium. If
her anorexia extends for a period of four or five years
or longer, a young woman's bones could resemble those
of a seventy-year-old, even though she may be only
twenty. At that point, simply walking can cause stress
fractures, and she'll be much more likely than average

to suffer from broken bones. Eventually osteoporosis can become incapacitating.

A lack of dietary protein can cause water retention, which is why many anorexics are dismayed to find their feet and legs swelling up with water. Poor intake of protein is also responsible for thin and brittle hair, anemia, lack of digestive enzymes (so that what is eaten often can't be assimilated), disturbed pancreatic function, and fatty liver (due to lack of proteins to carry fat out of the liver). The immune response will be greatly impaired because antibodies that normally protect the body have been broken down to provide amino acids. This means that infections can set in, including those that cause diarrhea, which further depletes the body of nutrients. Heart arrhythmias and heart failure can occur due to an imbalance in body salts (electrolytes), especially if the anorexic purges. In short, anorexia is extremely dangerous to one's health, and sometimes deadly.

The mortality rate for anorexia is higher than for any other psychiatric disorder. In fact, it's the number one cause of death in young women. Five to 10 percent of anorexics die within ten years of onset, 18 to 20 percent die within twenty years, and only 50 percent ever report being cured.[4] The most common causes of death among anorexics are starvation, suicide, and electrolyte imbalance (leading to heart failure).

What is bulimia nervosa?

Bulimia nervosa is characterized by *bingeing* and *purging*. The binge eating must be episodic—meaning that it occurs repeatedly (at least twice a week) for at least three months. During a binge, which usually takes place over the course of one to two hours, the individual feels completely out of control around food. Unable to stop herself, she eats huge quantities of primarily high-fat, high-sugar foods like cookies, cakes, and ice cream. She may eat other kinds of foods too, consuming as many as 50,000 calories during a single sitting.[5]

Once the binge is over, though, she is horrified at what she's done. Panic and guilt set in. To get rid of the calories, the bulimic will induce vomiting; take large amounts of laxatives or diuretics; engage in intense, prolonged periods of exercise; go on a rigid diet; or simply eat nothing at all. Bulimia, then, is a two-step process: first the binge, then the compensatory behavior. It is not simply overeating.

In spite of what most purgers might believe, purging is not an entirely effective means of getting rid of calories. Food moves quickly into the intestines and can't be regurgitated from there. And often some food will remain in the stomach even after vomiting. Laxatives do speed the food's transit time through the intestines, but many calories will still be absorbed. And diuretics increase only urination. While they may make a person feel thinner for a brief period of time, diuretics rid the body of only water and electrolytes; they don't affect fat. All in all, purging just doesn't work very well as a method of weight loss. That's why most bulimics are of average or above average weight.

Bulimics share the anorexic's intense fear of becoming fat, and body size or shape is extremely important to their self-esteem. But they can't see themselves objectively, so they never seem to feel that they're "thin enough." Slimness is an elusive goal—but that doesn't keep them from pursuing it.

What are the diagnostic criteria for bulimia nervosa?

Here's how the *DSM-IV* defines a person with bulimia nervosa:

- She has recurrent episodes of binge eating.
  Binge eating is defined as eating a larger amount of

food within a short period of time (two hours) than most people would eat in a similar period of time under similar circumstances, accompanied by the feeling that one cannot control what or how much is being eaten.

- She has recurrent episodes of compensatory behavior to avoid weight gain, such as *purging* (which includes self-induced vomiting and misuse of laxatives, diuretics, enemas, or other medications), fasting, or excessive exercise.

- She engages in binge eating and compensatory behaviors an average of *at least twice a week for three months.*

- Her self-worth depends on her body shape and weight.

- The bingeing and purging are *not* accompanied by anorexia nervosa (in which case she would be diagnosed as a binge eating/purging type of anorexic).

A Day in the Life of a Bulimic

April, a nineteen-year-old girl who lives with her parents, works as a secretary for a contractor. The contractor is out of the office for much of the day, leaving April to do the billing, type letters, answer the phone, and practice her bulimia. A typical day for April is as follows:

7:30 A.M.	Eats a full breakfast (eggs, toast, juice, hot chocolate).
8:00 A.M.	Vomits breakfast before walking to bus stop to catch bus to work. Carries a sack lunch including two sandwiches and a banana.
8:30 A.M.	On bus ride to work, eats the sandwiches and the banana.
9:00 A.M.	Arrives at work and promptly goes to the bathroom to relieve herself of the sandwiches and banana. Makes a quick trip to

	the small convenience store next door to buy a one-pound bag of jelly beans.
9:30 A.M.	Eats entire bag of jelly beans, then vomits them.
10:30 A.M.	Goes back to the store to buy a bag of cookies. Eats entire bag of cookies; vomits them.
11:30 A.M.	Goes back to the store to buy two or three candy bars. Eats them; vomits them.
12:30 P.M.	Lunchtime. Goes with friends to a local fast-food stand. Has a hamburger, soda, and french fries.
1:30 P.M.	Goes back to work; vomits lunch.
2:30 P.M.	Goes to the store to buy a couple of ice cream bars. Eats them; vomits them.
3:30 P.M.	Goes to the store for another bag of cookies or some candy bars. Eats them; vomits them.
4:30 P.M.	Goes to the store to buy a sandwich so she won't get hungry on the bus ride home.
5:00 P.M.	Leaves work; goes to bus stop. Eats sandwich while waiting for bus.
5:30 P.M.	Arrives home; vomits sandwich. Then has a couple pieces of bread, a slice of cheese, and an apple while waiting for dinner. Vomits them.
6:30 P.M.	Has dinner with family—spaghetti/meatballs, salad, bread, milk. Vomits all of it immediately afterward.
8:00 P.M.	Goes to nearby store; buys some candy bars. Eats them; vomits.
9:30 P.M.	Has a couple of ice cream bars before bed; vomits.

As you can see, April's entire life revolves around food. In fact, she can think of little else, which may be one of the functions that her eating disorder serves in her life. But what began as a "great weight-loss trick" quickly became addictive. By the time April arrived at an eating disorders clinic, her bulimia was so entrenched, she simply couldn't stop herself.

Bulimia is not only extremely detrimental to one's health, it's also exhausting and expensive. Bingeing and purging as many as twenty times a day is not uncommon. Some bulimics spend more than a hundred dollars a day on food, much of which ends up being vomited before the body can absorb its nutrients.

Is there more than one kind of bulimic?

Although bingeing and purging are two of the hallmarks of bulimia, that doesn't mean that all bulimics purge. There are two kinds of bulimics—the *purging type,* who compensate for bingeing by inducing vomiting or abusing laxatives, etc.; and the *nonpurging type,* who compensate by fasting or excessive exercising.

What's the definition of "excessive exercising"?

More than an hour of exercise per day *for the sole purpose of avoiding weight gain* is considered a compensatory behavior, and as many at 75 percent of anorexics and bulimics use exercise in this way.[6]

Christy Henrich, a world-class gymnast who died of anorexia at the age of twenty-two, was an extreme example of an excessive exerciser. She trained for three hours in the morning, and five more in the afternoon. Then, as soon as gymnastics practice was over, she hopped on the exercise bicycle and went full speed for another hour. Often she would also go for a five-mile run, either before or after practice. To fuel all this activity, she was eating exactly one apple a day—nothing more—which she eventually reduced to *one slice* of apple a day. At her lowest ebb, the 4'10" Henrich weighed 47 pounds.

How do you know when exercise has become "excessive exercise"?

The excessive exerciser engages in most (if not all) of these behaviors.

- She exercises more often and more intensely than is necessary for good health or performance excellence.
- She defines herself in terms of her performance.
- She is never satisfied with her performance.
- She takes more and more time away from work, school, or relationships to exercise.
- She is obsessed with weight and diet.

Although the excessive exerciser will insist that she has to lose weight to excel athletically, her real issues involve control, power, and self-esteem.

What are the physical consequences of bulimia?

Bingeing and purging are both harmful to the body. Bingeing can cause abnormal stretching or even rupture of the stomach, but purging is usually the more dangerous of the two behaviors. Self-induced vomiting can cause irritation or laceration of the esophagus, aspiration pneumonia if the vomitus is inhaled, and an imbalance of electrolytes that can lead to heart failure or other complications. The salivary glands can swell, giving the bulimic puffy "chipmunk cheeks." (Unfortunately, she often interprets this as a sign of overweight, so redoubles her dieting efforts.) The continual exposure to stomach acid causes tooth enamel to erode, giving the teeth a ragged "moth-eaten" look, and an increased number of dental cavities is also likely. Bulimics who induce vomiting often end up spending thousands of dollars getting their teeth capped.

Habitual use of ipecac, a drug used to induce vomiting, can destroy cardiac fibers, leading to heart dysfunction or failure. Chronic use of laxatives may paralyze the gut, making it unable to function. Other potential side effects of purging include vitamin and mineral deficiencies, chronic kidney problems, sinus infections, menstrual irregularities, dehydration, and broken blood vessels in the eyes or face.

We don't know how many people die of conditions related to bulimia, but some experts believe that the death rate may be as high as, or higher than, that for anorexia.[7]

Do bulimics know they're engaging in strange, destructive behavior?

Yes, and this is one characteristic that makes them different from anorexics. Although anorexics often can't see that their eating behavior is bizarre or dangerous, bulimics are usually painfully aware that their behavior is abnormal and out of control. That's one reason that depression, shame, and self-deprecation are commonly seen in bulimics.

In her book *Starving for Attention,* Cherry Boone O'Neill, daughter of singer Pat Boone, describes the particularly mortifying results of one of her binges. Her fiancé, Dan, had just dropped her off at home after a dinner date, and she had to pass through the kitchen on her way to her bedroom. Suddenly she spied the dog's dish sitting on the floor, piled high with leftovers from the family's dinner.

". . . the thought of the juicy marrow resting in the bone overwhelmed me. I couldn't stand the idea of those delectable morsels going to the dog. Without thinking, in the shadows of the laundry room . . . I impulsively squatted to the floor to feast on the dinner's remnants. . . . Soon I was ripping the meager remains from the bones, stuffing the cold meat into my mouth as fast as I could detach it. Suddenly, I heard a rap on the window behind me . . . Oh my God, no! It was Dan! He was standing at the back door watching me!"[8]

What other kinds of eating disorders are there?

Those with variations of anorexia and bulimia that are exceptions to the rule are considered to belong to the *DSM-IV*'s "Eating Disorders Not Otherwise Specified" category:

- *Those who have all the criteria for anorexia nervosa but are still menstruating.*
- *Those who have all the criteria for anorexia nervosa but whose weight remains in the normal range.* In most cases, they have already undergone significant weight loss. Chances are that the disorder is well under way, but they simply haven't lost enough weight to reach the critical stage—yet.
- *Those who binge/purge <u>less</u> than twice a week for three months.* There are those who binge and purge fairly regularly but don't do it twice a week for three months. Still, they exhibit the same impulsive behavior, "need" to eat voraciously, weight obsession, and depression found in diagnosed bulimics. Their bulimia may simply not have progressed to the point where it can be diagnosed as true bulimia nervosa, but they are certainly on the way and in need of treatment.
- *Those who purge after eating only small amounts of food.* Also known as purgers who don't binge, they are much more rare than bingers who don't purge (those with Binge Eating Disorder). Purgers who don't binge throw up, take laxatives, or exercise compulsively even though they have eaten only normal or below-normal amounts of food. The major difference between those in this category and the purging type of anorexic (who also purges even though she has eaten little food) is weight—the anorexic will be 85 percent or less of ideal body weight, while the purger who doesn't binge will be at or near normal weight.

- *Those who engage in oral expulsion.* This refers to those who chew food and spit it out rather than swallowing, to avoid calorie ingestion. These people have the obsession with weight and thinness, coupled with the overwhelming desire to eat seen in other eating disorders. A famous movie star has admitted using this method of weight control. She explained, "I'd go through a whole chocolate cake that way. I just wanted the taste—not the calories." Some people who engage in oral expulsion become addicted to it, spending hours chewing and spitting in secret. They can develop severe anxiety about swallowing and eventually find themselves unable to consume anything.

- *Those with Binge Eating Disorder (BED).* Formerly referred to as compulsive overeaters or food addicts, those with Binge Eating Disorder have many of the characteristics of bulimics. They voraciously consume huge amounts of food within a relatively short time (usually two hours) while experiencing the same out-of-control feelings. The difference is that those with BED don't purge.

Although not an officially recognized eating disorder, Binge Eating Disorder is much more common than either anorexia or bulimia. According to Dr. Christopher Fairburn, author of *Overcoming Binge Eating*, one in five young women reports that she has engaged in this kind of behavior.[9] Women are most likely to engage in this pattern of eating, but an estimated 40 percent of those with BED are male.[10] People who binge are condemned as "slobs" or "gluttons" who have no self-discipline or self-respect. The truth of the matter is that BED is produced by many of the same physical and psychological circumstances that bring on other eating disorders.

What are the diagnostic criteria for Binge Eating Disorder?

BED is not yet an "official" category of eating disorder, but the *DSM-IV* does list these diagnostic criteria as an aid to further research:

A. Recurrent episodes of binge eating. An episode of binge eating is characterized by both of the following:

1. Eating, in a discrete period of time (for example, within any two-hour period), an amount of food that is definitely larger than most people would eat in a similar period of time under similar circumstances; and

2. A sense of lack of control over eating during the episode (a feeling that one cannot stop eating or control what or how much one is eating).

B. The binge eating episodes are associated with three (or more) of the following:

1. Eating at a much more rapid pace than normal;

2. Eating until feeling uncomfortably full;

3. Eating large amounts of food when not feeling physically hungry;

4. Eating alone because of being embarrassed by how much one is eating;

5. Feeling disgusted with oneself, depressed, or very guilty after overeating.

C. Marked distress regarding binge eating is present.

D. The binge eating occurs, on average, at least two days a week for at least six months.[11]

E. The binge eating is not associated with the regular use of inappropriate compensatory behaviors (for example, purging, fasting, excessive exercise) and does not occur exclusively during the course of anorexia nervosa or bulimia nervosa.

Bingeing as a Way of Life

Janice was a typical victim of Binge Eating Disorder. Weighing in at 180 pounds, she was always trying to diet—and always failing. She just couldn't help herself. She'd start the day with black coffee, half of a grapefruit, and a bowl of whole grain cereal, but before she even left for work she'd be raiding the refrigerator. While at work she was usually "good" and rarely ate much in front of others for fear of being criticized. But once she got home, the free-for-all with food would begin.

"It's like I'm possessed or something. I open up the refrigerator and just start stuffing—it doesn't matter what. I just gobble up anything and everything I see. While I'm doing it, I'm sort of like in the twilight zone—I don't feel anything, I don't hear anything, I don't think about anything. But afterwards I always feel terrible. I know I'm not supposed to eat like that, and I know I'll never lose weight that way. But I can't seem to help it—it just happens."

What are the signs of an eating disorder in progress?

Any of the following can be an indication of anorexia, bulimia, or another eating disorder in progress:

1. The individual is preoccupied with her weight, food, diets, and calories.
2. Her weight has dropped to an abnormally low point.
3. She eats a great deal but never seems to gain weight.
4. She makes excuses for not eating.
5. She divides foods or behaviors into clear-cut "good" or "bad" categories.
6. She often goes to the bathroom right after meals

and sometimes stays there for a prolonged period of time (say, longer than ten minutes).

7. Her eyes are often bloodshot.

8. She often complains about "being fat."

9. Quantities of food have been mysteriously disappearing from the cupboard or the refrigerator.

10. She wears loose-fitting clothes that hide her figure.

11. She is moody or irritable for no reason.

12. She is often angry or depressed without just cause.

13. She is unreasonable or illogical about certain foods, which she refuses to eat.

14. She fasts regularly.

15. She is often tired or low on energy.

16. There is swelling in the glands of her neck or face.

17. There are scrape wounds on the backs of her knuckles (due to contact between knuckles and the front teeth when inducing vomiting).

18. She is often cold.

19. She often has trouble sleeping and gets up at night.

20. It seems like you never actually see her eat anything.

21. She takes laxatives or gives herself enemas more often than once in a while.

22. There are signs that she's been vomiting even when she's not sick.

23. She often cooks or bakes foods for other people but refuses to eat these foods herself.

24. The dentist has reported that her tooth enamel is eroding or that she is getting more cavities.

25. She consumes a lot of noncaloric foods such as diet soda, coffee, mustard, gum, or spices.

26. She seems to use food to reward herself.

27. She obsessively counts every calorie.

28. Her hair is falling out or looking dry and brittle.

29. She is defensive about her weight.
30. She spends money but doesn't seem to have anything to show for it.
31. She panics when she can't weigh herself.
32. She performs an exhausting, excessive exercise routine to "burn off" the calories she's eaten.
33. She alternates between severely restricting her eating and eating large quantities of food.
34. Her weight seems to go up and down in dramatic fluctuations of ten pounds or more.
35. Her menstrual cycle is irregular for no discernible reason.
36. She is extremely concerned about her appearance, which is the defining feature of her self-esteem.
37. She is pale and complains of light-headedness.

How many people are affected by eating disorders?

According to the National Association of Anorexia Nervosa and Associated Disorders (ANAD), approximately eight million Americans are affected by anorexia and bulimia, and nine out of ten of them are girls or women. Throughout the world, anorexia is seen almost exclusively in industrialized societies where there is plenty of food and a primary element of female attractiveness is thinness. This disease occurs primarily in the United States, Europe, Canada, Australia, New Zealand, Japan, and South Africa. In the United States alone, a whopping 15 percent of the country's one million girls and young women exhibit substantially disordered eating behaviors and attitudes.[12] One percent actually meet the diagnostic criteria for anorexia, and another 1 to 3 percent for bulimia.[13]

Although statistics on Binge Eating Disorder are scarce, current estimates from the National Institutes of Health suggest that 2 percent of all adults, or one to two million Americans, suffer from BED. Women are 1.5 times more likely to develop this disorder than men and, in either sex, most are obese or severely obese. Onset of BED usually occurs during late adolescence or the early twenties, often right after a significant weight loss. Some experts estimate that 20 to 40 percent of those in weight-reduction programs may suffer from BED.[14]

At approximately what age does an eating disorder begin? And how long does it take someone to recover?

The average age of onset of anorexia is seventeen; it almost always begins by age twenty, and rarely occurs after forty. Some individuals may suffer through just a single episode of anorexia, then recover. Others may gain weight and relapse several times before recovering, but many find themselves on a downhill course that lasts for several years, resulting in serious disability or even death. About half of the anorexic population will eventually develop bulimia (sometimes referred to as failed anorexia) when the overwhelming urge to eat gives way to bingeing and its compensatory behaviors.

Bulimia is more common than anorexia, with onset usually occurring in the late teens or early twenties. Like anorexia, it is a disease found primarily in industrialized nations, and 90 percent of its victims are female. It strikes college-aged women particularly hard; experts estimate that one out of four college women uses bingeing and purging as a method of weight control.[15] Female college athletes are at even greater risk, with one out of three admitting to bingeing and purging in an attempt to improve athletic performance by controlling weight.[16] The American College of Sports Medicine estimates that among girls and women who compete in "appearance sports" (gymnastics, figure skating, etc.), some 62 percent have some sort of eating disorder.

Once bulimia takes hold, it often lasts for several years. There is no consensus on the rates of cure for eating disorders, partly because there is a lot of leeway in diagnosis and partly because many people don't seek treatment. But among bulimics who were ill enough to require hospitalization, studies done three years after treatment showed that 27 percent had good outcomes (meaning they binged/purged less than one time a month), while 33 percent had poor outcomes (meaning they still binged/purged on a daily basis). The remaining 40 percent had outcomes somewhere between good and poor.[17]

Now that we have defined the various eating disorders and are aware of some of the physical signs that indicate trouble, let's take a look at one of the factors that help make them such a widespread problem: society's attitude toward the overweight.

Chapter Two

WEIGHT LOSS: OUR NATIONAL OBSESSION

In early adolescence, girls learn how important appearance is in defining social acceptability. Attractiveness is both a necessary and a sufficient condition for girls' success. This is an old, old problem. Helen of Troy didn't launch a thousand ships because she was a hard worker. Juliet wasn't loved for her math ability.

—Mary Pipher,
Reviving Ophelia

Over the past hundred years, society has done a terrible disservice to girls and women by inextricably linking feminine beauty to a slender body. This has given them the mistaken impression that to be loved, valued, successful, and attractive, they need to be slim. Beginning as far back as the turn of the century, many women have responded to this pressure by dieting and exercising in hopes of attaining the "ideal shape." They believed (and many still do believe) that the mind could will the body to take on an entirely new form—even one that was totally unnatural. They learned dieting "tricks" such as starving and purging. But Mother Nature was (and is) a formidable opponent in the weight-loss game, one who triggers binges and slows the metabolism to effectively keep most body weight firmly in place. Women have found themselves between a rock and a hard place—society compels them to be thin, but Mother Nature finds ways to keep them at their natural weight.

Still, society won't let up. In fact, as the years have rolled by, the "ideal shape," a concept widely promoted by the media, has become thinner and thinner. (Miss Sweden of 1951 was 5'7" and 151 pounds; Miss Sweden of 1983 was 5'9" and 109 pounds.)[1] Today it's practically impossible to achieve the dangerous levels of thinness glamorized in magazines, on television, or in the movies while maintaining good health. Unfortunately, too many girls and young women are trying to do just that.

This is not to say that *all* changes in diet or exercise habits are unhealthful or dangerous. For some people, small changes in these areas can be wise and healthful strategies—*if* they're done in moderation and *if* extra pounds are due to gobbling too many goodies or sitting in front of the TV too long. But if dieting or exercising is taken to an extreme, or if the dieter is trying to sculpt an entirely new body shape that Mother Nature never intended, problems can arise. Both mind and body may revolt—and the result is often the development of a full-blown eating disorder.

Racing to Lose Weight

To shave a few seconds off her racing time, world-class runner Ellen Hart Pena dieted her way from 132 pounds to 110 pounds—an unnaturally low weight for her 5'5" frame. Her body, however, refused to be manipulated without a fight, sending forth powerful hunger signals that couldn't be ignored.

". . . I'd have this uncontrollable urge to eat ice cream, cookies, doughnuts—anything high calorie. And I'd eat until I couldn't eat anymore. Afterward, I couldn't bear the thought that it would stay in me and turn into fat, so I'd have to purge. During the worst periods, I'd binge and purge four or five times a day, from the moment I woke up until I went to sleep. . . . [Eventually] I was down to 110 and I looked like a cadaver."

Ellen continued to be plagued with bulimia for the

next ten years. "I used my body as a battleground," she said. "Food was my weapon." With the help of therapy, she finally stopped forcing her body to assume an unnatural weight and shape. Today, at a healthy 125 pounds, she is able to resist the occasional temptation to binge and purge. Now the mother of two children, Ellen refuses to get back on the dieting merry-go-round, saying, "I'm not walking near that cliff again because going over the edge was my private hell. I can't go back."[2]

How do I know if I really have a weight problem or I'm just trying to make my body look a certain way?

To answer this question, we'll need to define four terms: *overweight*, *overfat*, *obese*, and *Body Mass Index (BMI)*.

Overweight simply means that you weigh at least 10 percent more than is recommended for your height, frame, and age, but that isn't a reliable sign that you've got a health problem. Muscle tissue weighs more than fat, so if you are a body builder or an athlete or simply have a genetic predisposition to putting on muscle, being overweight may be perfectly healthy for you. That's why looking at weight charts or hopping on the scale isn't the best way to determine whether you need to lose weight.

Overfat is the presence of too much body fat, which can occur not only in overweight people but also in those of normal weight. For example, even though she may look lean, a skinny model may actually be overfat if she doesn't exercise enough and has a low percentage of muscle mass. Weighing yourself won't tell you if you've got too much body fat. Your *body fat percentage* is a much more accurate indication of a possible health problem.

Recommended body fat percentages are 20 to 30 percent for women and 12 to 20 percent for men.[3] Be aware that a very *low* body fat percentage can be just as dangerous as one that's too high, since it suggests that the body is in a starvation state. Women who dip much below 18 percent can develop a hormone imbalance that results in osteoporosis (the thinning of the bones) and the loss of menstruation (amenorrhea). Some long-term anorexics end up with bones that are as thin and brittle as those of a seventy-year-old woman. Kidney dysfunction and liver problems are also side effects of eating too little food for too long.

The most accurate method of determining body fat percentage is hydrostatic (underwater) weighing, but it can also be determined by measuring a fold of skin with special calipers; passing a painless, low-energy electrical current through the body; measuring the amount of radioactive potassium that the body emits; or using in-frared light. Ask your doctor how and where you can get an accurate assessment of your body fat percentage.

Obesity is defined by some experts as being more than 20 percent over the recommended weight for a person's height, frame, and age, but as you know, poundage alone isn't an accurate assessment of health. Others define obesity as more than 20 percent body fat in men and more than 30 percent body fat in women. A third definition, more accurate than the other two, in-volves the *BMI*, or *Body Mass Index*. Your doctor or a clinician can calculate this for you—or you can figure it yourself. (See box.)

Figuring Your Body Mass Index

1. Convert your weight to kilograms by dividing the pounds by 2.2.
2. Convert your height to meters by dividing the inches by 39.4. Then square your answer by multiplying it by itself.
3. Divide your answer to #1 by your answer to #2. This is your Body Mass Index (BMI).

Example: What is the BMI for a 5'4" woman who weighs 120 pounds?

1. 120 lb. ÷ 2.2 = 54.5 kilograms
2. 64" ÷ 39.4 = 1.6 meters; then 1.6 × 1.6 = 2.56
3. 54.5 ÷ 2.56 = **21.3**

For men: A BMI of 22–24 is desirable; more than 28.5 is overweight; more than 33 is obese.
For women: A BMI of 21–23 is desirable; more than 27.5 is overweight; more than 31.5 is obese.

Note: The BMI should not be applied to children, adolescents who are still growing, adults over sixty-five, pregnant or lactating women, or those who are very muscular.

If you want to know if you truly have a "weight problem" and aren't just trying to conform to some impossible aesthetic standards, figure your BMI and ask your doctor to determine your body fat percentage. If these figures are higher than recommended, stepping up your activity level and cutting back on high-calorie foods may be indicated. But do so with *moderation,* and forget the notion of ideal weight. Your goal should be to achieve the best weight possible *within the context of good health.* And remember a BMI or body fat percentage that is too low can also indicate a problem. See a doctor if you're outside the desirable range for either of these measurements.

What makes one person more likely to develop a weight problem than another person?

Any of the following factors can contribute to the likelihood that you will become obese.[4]

* Heredity
* Being female

- Overfeeding during infancy, adolescence, or pregnancy
- Significant overeating for a long period of time
- Using food as a reward or to relieve stress or depression
- Being a first- or second-generation American
- Dieting

About heredity—both of my parents are heavy. Does that mean I'm going to be heavy too?

Not necessarily, although the odds are good. A child who has one obese parent stands a 40 percent chance of becoming obese. The child of two obese parents, however, has an 80 percent chance. The size and location of the fat deposits, bone size, metabolism, and other factors are all determined by heredity, so if your parents were large, you'll probably be large, too.

Heavy people also tend to have less *brown fat*, a special kind of fatty tissue that helps to raise the body temperature slightly and burn off excess calories. While a thin body may be able to burn off an extra load of calories quickly, an overweight body is often genetically programmed to be "thrifty," saving every last calorie. We've all heard the complaint "She eats all day long and never gains any weight. I eat one cookie and gain two pounds!" Brown fat may be at least part of the reason.

You can't change your genetic legacy. But rather than trying to become something or someone you were never intended to be, why not concentrate on becoming as healthy as possible, through good nutrition and moderate, regular exercise? Radiant good health is the most attractive thing that anyone can wear, while poor health, even on a "perfect" body, is anything but pretty.

Why are females more likely to become obese?

Females are genetically programmed to carry greater amounts of fat—for reproductive reasons, for insulation, and to provide a ready supply of calories for breast-feeding an infant. Females most likely to put on extra fatty tissue at certain well-defined times in their lives—during infancy (when many fat cells are formed), during puberty (when body fat must reach approximately 20 percent for menstruation to begin), and during pregnancy (when fatty tissue is added so there will be sufficient calories for milk production once the baby arrives). But it also appears that fat generates fat—that is, the more fat cells a person has, the more efficient the body becomes at producing and storing them. So females (who are genetically programmed to carry more fat than males) tend to be especially good at both generating and holding on to fat deposits.

Males, on the other hand, have greater amounts of lean body tissue (muscle), which is more metabolically active than fatty tissue (meaning that it burns more calories, even in the resting state). As a result, the average man has a higher metabolic rate and burns off calories *faster* than the average woman. The upshot of all of this is that women are more likely to become obese than men, a fact that becomes even more apparent as we age. Among older people (age sixty-five and above), *one half* of the women are obese compared with one third of the men.

How can overfeeding during infancy contribute to obesity?

The majority of fat cells are formed during the first two years of life. Overfeeding during this crucial time period can cause an abnormally high number of fat cells to be created. Once laid down, fat cells function by swelling up during times when food is plentiful, then shrinking during times of famine as the fatty acids are withdrawn and used for fuel. But even when food intake has been restricted for a long period of time, these fat cells never disappear. They simply lie dormant and wait for their chance to inflate again. An infant who is overfed, then, creates an excess number of fat cells that she's stuck with for the rest of her life.

To make matter worse, greater amounts of fat cells inspire greater amounts of hunger. So the person carrying a large number of fat cells is actually fighting a double battle when she tries to lose weight: she has fat cells that won't go away, plus abnormal hunger. One study found that the number of fat cells a person has is a good predictor of how successful she will be at losing weight.[5]

How does overfeeding during adolescence or pregnancy contribute to the likelihood of obesity?

During adolescence and pregnancy, a girl or woman will gain body fat even faster than she gains lean tissue, so overfeeding can have disastrous consequences. Many will find that the weight they gain during these periods stays with them for life. If she can get through these periods without gaining an excessive amount of weight, her chances of becoming obese will be markedly reduced. Therefore, good nutrition and moderate, regular exercise during adolescence and pregnancy can be critical for the prevention of obesity.

Does overeating over a long period of time make new fat cells appear?

At one time, experts believed that once the fat cells had been laid down (around the age of two), they simply swelled and shrank in response to the food supply. Now many researchers in the field believe that new fat cells *can* be created in the presence of continual overfeeding. This makes sense when you consider that some morbidly obese people tip the scales at 800 or 1,000 pounds.

What part do stress and depression play in obesity?

People who feel stressed, anxious, depressed, bored, or otherwise out of sorts may turn to food in an attempt to soothe themselves. Foods high in carbohydrate (especially sugary foods) may be favored—partly because of the taste, but also because carbohydrate stimulates the brain to secrete a brain chemical called *serotonin*. Serotonin brings about feelings of well-being, tranquillity, sleepiness, and satisfaction. To those who get "hooked" on the effects of serotonin, eating can become a conditioned response to just about any emotional state—euphoria, depression, anger, etc. To them, food may be a kind of cure-all when they feel bad, and a way to feel even better when they feel good.

How does being a first- or second-generation American figure in to the obesity problem?

Poverty, cultural values, and cultural adjustments all seem to play a role in the development of obesity. Immigrants often have little money and are exposed to extreme amounts of stress as they try to learn the language and fit into a new culture. They may be attracted to cheap, high-calorie fast foods; they may take refuge in eating to soothe themselves; or they may come from cultures that favor heaviness as a sign of prosperity.

Why would dieting make me more likely to become obese?

Many experts believe that each of us is programmed with a "set point" for body fat. You can think of the set point as a sort of thermostat for fat deposits. If the body fat gets too low, the thermostat shifts on and starts conserving calories. Too much body fat, on the other hand, shuts the thermostat off so that excess calories can be burned more easily.

The set point may be one reason we see so many differences in body types. We've all known people who seem to eat like crazy and never gain a pound—their set points for body fat may be quite low. Their body fat may have to drop to a very low point before their bodies start actively conserving and storing calories. On the other hand, some overweight or obese people may have extremely high set points. It seems that no matter how little fat they've stored, their bodies continue to conserve calories.

When the food supply is curtailed (as it is during dieting), the body believes that it's undergoing a famine and automatically goes into its calorie-conservation mode. It burns calories much more slowly, raising its normal set point to a *higher* level for the next time. That means it will take longer than ever before to switch from slow burning to fast burning. For example, let's say your metabolism burns calories at a fast rate as long as you're eating at least 1,200 calories a day but goes into its slow mode if you drop down below 1,200. After you follow a low-calorie diet (say, below 1,200 calories), your body may begin to shift into its calorie-conserving mode if you eat less than 1,500 calories a day. By restricting your food intake, you've effectively *raised* your set point and trained your body to be a slow calorie burner. Like a miser counting his pennies, your body will hold on to its energy supply rather than burn calories in its former, more "wasteful" way.

Besides raising your set point, dieting reduces the amount of muscle tissue that your body carries. Muscle tissue is more metabolically active than fatty tissue (it takes more calories to keep a muscle cell alive than a fat cell), so if you reduce the amount of muscle you've got, you'll automatically reduce your calorie requirement too. This means that to *maintain your weight*, you'll have to eat *less* than ever before. So after dieting, not only is your body burning calories at a lower rate, your calorie requirement drops too! Is it any wonder that only one in nine dieters manages to maintain her weight loss once the diet is over?

Does dieting do anything else to make me fatter?

Yes—it makes you hungry! Restrictive (low-calorie) diets cause your body to release greater amounts of insulin, which increase your appetite and *help maintain it* even when your stomach is already full. Your body, believing there's a famine, wants you to be able to eat whenever you get the opportunity—even if you've just eaten!

So dieting can bring about three counterproductive results: a slower metabolic rate, a lower calorie requirement, and an increase in hunger. The unhappy outcome: You can end up even fatter than you were *before* you dieted! There's even a formal term for this: "diet-induced obesity."

In spite of all this, Americans are some of the most avid dieters in the world. We've taken amphetamines and appetite suppressants; we've had our stomachs stapled, our jaws wired shut, and the fat sucked out of our bodies through liposuction. We've followed one-food diets, liquid diets, high-protein/low-carbohydrate diets, diets made up of magic food combinations, and diets that required us to drink gallons of water each day. We've joined health clubs, taken steam baths, and sweated through aerobics classes. We've spent incredible sums of money (one expert estimates that it's close to $50 billion a year)[6] trying to get slim and stay that way. And in spite of all that, the average American adult has *gained* eight pounds in the last decade.[7] Because as just about any dieter can tell you, diets don't work—at least not for long. (See Chapter 4 for more on diets.)

When did America's obsession with thinness begin?

For centuries a woman's worth has been defined in terms of her beauty, but thinness as a necessary ingredient of female attractiveness didn't become mandatory until the Flapper Era in the 1920s. Back in the eighteenth and nineteenth centuries, plump cheeks and arms, a full bosom, and ample hips were considered attractive indications of upper-class status—a woman with these qualities was obviously well fed and didn't have to do physical work.

But between the 1880s and the 1920s, when food became plentiful and almost everyone had enough to eat, plumpness began to get a reputation as unhealthful. It became even less desirable as more immigrants of sturdy peasant stock began to arrive in America. In an effort to distinguish themselves from the lower classes, upper-class people began to emulate the European model of refinement, which was slender. Heaviness was déclassé. Soon, thinness not only became aesthetically desirable and a symbol of one's good breeding but was also considered "morally superior" to heaviness. Slenderness was associated with self-discipline, self-denial, and self-control, while heaviness signaled gluttony, greed, and slothfulness.

At the turn of the century, the plump Victorian body gave way to a more athletic (although still curvy) figure that was idealized in drawings of the Gibson girl. The Gibson girl was dreamed up by Charles Dana Gibson, a magazine illustrator who based his creation on the upper-class, well-to-do young women with whom he played tennis—or, that is, an idealized version of them. With her taller, slimmer build, slightly broad shoulders, and very tiny waist, the Gibson girl looked like no one in existence—because she didn't *really* exist herself! But she became so popular that her image was used by advertisers to sell everything from corsets to face cream. Soon anything "endorsed" by the Gibson girl began to sell like hotcakes. Americans were enthralled by her appearance, and for the first time women started to feel somewhat self-conscious about their own looks. *They* didn't look like the Gibson girl; maybe that meant there was something wrong with them. The fact that *no one* looked like the Gibson girl seemed to escape the notice of women all over the country who tried to emulate her idealized face and figure.

Around this time, Americans embraced a new fad—physical fitness. Hailed as a remedy for "whatever ailed you"—be it corpulence, hysteria, or nervous disorders—bicycling, rowing, tennis, and calisthenics became extremely popular. But this new level of activity demanded less constricting clothes. As a result, corsets loosened up; women began to wear shorter skirts that showed their ankles, and sometimes (for bicycling) they even wore "knickerbockers" (divided skirts that resembled bloomers). After centuries of being swathed, draped, encircled, or otherwise camouflaged, the body finally began to emerge from its clothing constraints. As fashions revealed more than ever before, women became more self-conscious about their bodies. "Flaws" that would have been well concealed in the past were suddenly out there for all to see. To make matters worse, insurance companies started to make up charts of ideal weights for men and women. Americans began to believe in the idea of a "perfect form" and that by watching what they ate and getting plenty of exercise, they could achieve it.

In 1908 the straight, slim Empire-waisted dress came into vogue. But it looked "right" only on a slender, small-breasted body, and soon women throughout the country became anxious about having too many curves. The raising of the hemlines to mid-calf in the mid-1920s only increased their anxiety—now even legs were visible. There was no way to hide any "excess baggage." Women were desperate to acquire the new "flapper look"—slim, petite, and flat chested—and were willing to wage war on their bodies to get it.

By this time corsets had been permanently flung aside, so "figure control" relied on interior methods rather than exterior ones. For the first time in history, fad diets, prolonged fasting, vomiting, bizarre food combinations, and laxative use became the mode.

> "Don't you want to be thin? This is the age of the figure. The face alone, no matter how pretty, counts for nothing unless the body is straight and yielding as every young girl's."
>
> —*Delineator* magazine,[8]
> April 1914

Advertisers in the twenties began to prey on women's insecurity about their too-full figures, featuring illustrations of slim, beautiful women in ads for weight-loss aids such as bath salts, "stimulating" brushes, laxatives, reducing belts, diets-through-the-mail, and other slimming gadgets. Some ads used guilt or humiliation to make their point, and all of them implied or even outright promised that a woman's life would be much improved once she became more slender.

> "Overweight these days is a woman's own fault."
>
> —Ad for a musical reducing record,[9]
> circa 1920

Did the pressure to be thin ease up after the twenties?

For the most part, no. With the advent of the movie industry, Hollywood movie stars became the icons of beauty and style, emulated by millions of young women throughout the country. These stars, handpicked by the studios for their uncommon beauty, were required to be thinner than normal since the camera tended to add pounds. So the average woman began to compare herself with women who were not only unusually beautiful but also unusually thin. It was no longer enough for a girl to be the prettiest in her class or to have a gorgeous head of hair. If she didn't "measure up" to Jean Harlow, she felt inadequate. But while she might not be able to change her facial features, she figured that she *could* do something about her weight. Thus all across the country, the dieting craze began to gather steam.

In the 1940s, fashion designers favored slim skirts and heavily padded shoulders to accentuate a small waist. But to show off their designs properly, the designers realized that they needed very slim models. Too many curves disturbed the "hang" of the clothing, so they recruited unnaturally thin models to display their fashions. Soon women's magazines were full of images of long, lean nymphlike creatures whose bodies intruded so little on the lines of the clothes that they might just as well have been hangers. The message was clear: If you want to be fashionable, you'd better be slim.

During the fifties a lusher, fuller, more buxom body (epitomized by Marilyn Monroe) briefly came into style. You might think that women could finally heave a sigh of relief, but the Marilyn Monroe–style body was a hard one to achieve. Although it was very voluptuous on top and bottom, a small waist and long, slim legs were still de rigueur. This was also the era in which little girls were introduced to a brand-new "role model" whose proportions they could one day hope to emulate—the Barbie doll. Barbie, with her impossibly long legs, large breasts, and minuscule waist, would actually measure 36-18-33 if she were life-size.[10] But little girls didn't know that—they just assumed that Barbie was what big girls looked like and one day they'd look like that too. Nine out of ten girls would eventually own at least one Barbie doll, firmly implanting the thinness ideal into their impressionable minds.

When did thinness become idealized in the United States?

The 1960s saw a fashion revolution that was similar to the one that had occurred in the twenties when corsets (this time girdles) had permanently been tossed aside and hemlines had been raised to scandalous heights. The body and its accompanying defects were revealed for all to see—raising body consciousness to an all-time high. In 1966, American women had a new reason to feel less than adequate: the new darling of the fashion world was a 5'6", 95-pound teenager named Twiggy who measured 31-22-32. Yes, thin was definitely in, and Marilyn Monroe's brief era of voluptuous curves had disappeared into thin air.

The American woman's drive for thinness continued to gain momentum through the sixties and into the seventies, when the saying "You can never be too thin or too rich" could have been the motto of the majority of the nation's young females. With the advent of women's liberation, women were out in the workplace in record numbers, competing with men at higher levels than ever before. Curvaceousness and overt femininity were undesirable traits for a woman who was jockeying for power in a male-dominated world. A more mannish or at least androgynous physique was preferred—one that was broad shouldered, slim hipped, and fairly flat chested. Women needed the kind of body that looked good in a jacket and trousers—in other words, *not* your average female body. Once again they got the message: Your body is not okay.

About the same time, the "fitness" craze began to sweep the nation, spearheaded by actress Jane Fonda. No longer was it enough just to get some fresh air and exercise on a regular basis. Women now felt obliged to acquire a perfectly toned, slim, well-disciplined physique through hours of daily exercise. The goal was to look like Fonda herself—slender, with a perfectly flat stomach and thin thighs, and absolutely firm every-where. That was a body that maybe 2 percent of American women could hope to achieve. (Later we would find out that Jane Fonda, our idol, had been a practicing bulimic for some twenty years, and that she sometimes threw up as often as twenty times a day!) So now women weren't just expected to be thin, thin, thin but also firm, firm, firm. Was it any wonder that it had become next to impossible to find a woman who really *liked* her own body?

> "There is a huge gap between the reality of our own bodies and the images to which we aspire. . . . Yet we continue to go for the image. And business gladly serves us in this chase as long as it continues to be profitable."
>
> —Sharlene Hesse-Biber,
> *Am I Thin Enough Yet?*

With the death of Karen Carpenter in the early eighties, the American public first began to become aware of the growing problem of eating disorders among young girls and women. Celebrities like Jane Fonda, Sally Field, Lynn Redgrave, and even Britain's Princess Diana eventually "came out of the closet" with stories of their own struggles with anorexia or bulimia. Eating disorder clinics sprang up around the country, and magazines regularly featured articles on the warning signs of these illnesses and what to do if a loved one developed eating problems.

Did this change society's attitude toward unnatural thinness?

In a fairy tale, we would be able to tell you triumphantly that this was the turning point in our cultural obsession with "the body beautiful"—and that we have now returned to appreciating the female form in its more natural state. Unfortunately the reverse is true. In 1972, 23 percent of American women were dissatisfied with their overall appearance. In 1996, 48 percent expressed that sentiment.[11] According to a poll done by *People* magazine in 1996, women were three times more likely than men to have negative feelings about their bodies; and the younger the woman, the more unhappy she was.[12]

The incidence of both anorexia and bulimia has steadily increased in the last decade. Studies done in Britain, the United States, and Australia have shown that as many as one third of adolescent girls try fasting to control their weight, one third binge eat at least occasionally, and one tenth induce vomiting.[13] Then there are the girls and young women who use cocaine or crack to control their weight. Vicki Greenleaf, author of *Women and Cocaine*, notes that many young women find cocaine to be "the perfect, ladylike drug . . . It's slimming, it's sensual and you don't slur your words. You can carry it around in your cosmetic case just like a lipstick."[14] Never mind that it is highly addictive and can cause delusions, hallucinations, hyperactivity, insomnia, and anxiety disorders. It can make you thin.

The physical fitness craze seems to have gone to extremes too. Female bodybuilders, with their bulging biceps and thighs, veined forearms, and tiny waists, have become almost commonplace in local gyms. Through their exhaustive, compulsive exercising, the reduction of body fat to dangerously low levels, and (often) the use of male hormones, these women have succeeded in erasing just about every trace of their "femaleness." Rather than being the champions of the female body by taking it to new heights, as they claim, they may well be the group that loathes the natural womanly form the most. But as we've seen, one certainly doesn't have to be a bodybuilder to share this attitude.

Many "average" women have also become compulsive exercisers, trying to achieve the rippling abdominals and super-defined upper arms that used to be seen only in men. "I want to get that 'cut' in my upper arms," says Alissa, a twenty-year-old college student who spends three to four hours a day at the gym. "I think really strong arms on a woman are sexy." Never mind that estrogen and natural patterns of fat deposition work against this look. Alissa decided that she wanted to dedicate the majority of her free time—time that might be spent studying, socializing, reading, or engaging in artistic endeavors—on achieving "the look."

So it's society's fault that so many people have eating disorders?

No, society's attitude toward the female body is just part of the problem. If living in a "thin-is-in" world were all it took, *all* young girls would develop eating disorders, instead of just a small percentage. But society's emphasis on thinness does provide a breeding ground for the development of "body loathing." After all, eating disorders have become a serious problem only since the "thinness mania" overtook our society some twenty-five to thirty years ago.

Only when we can finally reject unnatural thinness as a worthy goal can we create a society in which women can feel good about their bodies and themselves. Right now *a full 95 percent of American women report disappointment with their bodies*. Is it at all surprising that some will resort to desperate measures like starving, stuffing, or purging to gain acceptance? Eating disorders are a symptom of a condition that plagues almost all women today: the feeling that they're not good enough. As a society we need to relearn that there is much beauty to be found in the natural female form. Until we do, eating disorders will continue to affect the health and sanity of countless girls and young women, sometimes to the point of death.

How can I tell if I have an eating disorder?

Just for starters, take the following quiz, marking each sentence "True" or "False."

___ 1. I often feel fat, even though people keep telling me I'm thin.

___ 2. The first thing I think about when I wake up in the morning is food.

___ 3. I feel uneasy about food and eating, but I keep my feelings to myself because no one would understand.

___ 4. I have dieted to an abnormally low weight because that makes me feel like I'm in control.

___ 5. I haven't had a menstrual period for at least the past three months.

___ 6. I often eat when I'm not hungry.

___ 7. My greatest fear is that I'll gain weight and become fat.

___ 8. I can't go through a day without worrying about what I can or cannot eat.

___ 9. I have had an out-of-control eating binge at least once during the past year.

___ 10. I often eat until I'm so full I feel uncomfortable.

___ 11. I have done one of the following after a binge at least once during the past year: made myself vomit; used laxatives, enemas, colonics, or diuretics; fasted; exercised excessively.

___ 12. If I got on the scale tomorrow and found that I'd gained two pounds, I'd be very upset.

___ 13. If I can't exercise to compensate for food I have eaten, I panic.

___ 14. I push food around on my plate so that it looks like I'm eating more than I really am.

___ 15. Often I eat to make myself feel better emotionally, but then I feel guilty about it.

___ 16. I prefer to eat little in public; then I binge secretly in private.

___ 17. I think and talk a lot about food, recipes, weight, diets, restaurants, and other topics related to food.

___ 18. People always seem to be bothering me about what I'm eating or not eating, which makes me angry.

___ 19. I don't believe I'll be able to find happiness until I'm thin.

___ 20. It's important to me to be thinner than my friends.

If you've marked *any* of the above questions "True" (especially questions 4, 5, 7, 8, 11, 13, 16, or 19), you may have an eating problem. Make an appointment today with your physician for a thorough checkup. He or she may also refer you to a psychologist or a psychiatrist and a registered dietitian trained in eating disorders. If you're in school, see your school nurse, counselor, ombudsman, or other student support personnel. You can also contact your local mental health association or any of the resources listed in Appendix 2. The most important thing is to get help *now*. Eating disorders become more difficult to treat the longer they last. Early intervention is invaluable—and the best hope for achieving a lifelong cure.

Chapter Three

ANATOMY OF AN EATING DISORDER: WHAT CAUSES IT AND WHO'S AT RISK?

I do not remember that I did ever in all my Practice see one that was conversant with the Living so much wasted . . . (like a Skeleton only clad with Skin) . . .

—Richard Morton, English physician, describing a case of anorexia nervosa, 1689

Twenty-two-year-old Jeri was the last person you'd ever expect to develop an eating disorder. Intelligent, vivacious, and blessed with a movie star's good looks, she was by far the most popular girl at the small southern college she attended. "Jeri had the perfect life," said her roommate, Georgia. "Everybody loved her; she got really good grades, had a perfect figure and the clothes to show it off, and was voted cheerleader in her freshman year. On top of that, she ended up engaged to the cutest guy in the school. There wasn't anybody who wouldn't have traded their life for hers in a second."

But after living with Jeri for a couple of months, Georgia began to notice that her friend often seemed tired and depressed. Georgia figured it must be because of the crazy diets Jeri was always on. "Jeri was constantly on one diet or another, even though she had the perfect figure," Georgia mused. "And she was really driving herself to drop another five pounds—although she certainly didn't need to. The funny thing was, even though Jeri ate next to nothing, my food kept disappearing from the refrigerator. When I'd ask her about it, she'd say that her boyfriend ate it and she'd pay me back. Then I started noticing that Jeri often spent a long time in the bathroom right after she'd eaten something. It took me a while, but I finally realized that she was throwing up practically everything she ate.

"The thing I couldn't understand was why somebody who had absolutely everything going for her would get caught up in an eating disorder. She wasn't even fat! Why in the world did it happen to *her*?"

Why do eating disorders happen?
Are specific groups more at risk?

Eating disorders are caused by a host of factors, including certain personality traits, ways of thinking, genetic legacies, family dynamics, and stages of life, that when combined can cause an apparently "normal" person to turn on herself and her body. Later we'll discuss these factors in detail, but first let's take a look at certain specific groups that are particularly at risk for developing eating disorders:

• *Teenage girls and young women from white upper-middle-class homes (anorexia)*
Dr. Hilde Bruch, who successfully treated anorexics beginning in the early 1970s until her death in 1986, likened these young women to birds trapped in a "golden cage." Her patients often came from well-to-do families of high social position and were given every material thing they could ever want or need. Their parents were likely to place a great deal of importance on appearance—everyone in the family was always expected to look good and exhibit all the social graces. A girl from such a family may feel extreme pressure to live up to (or even exceed) family expectations. At the same

time, she is plagued with a deep sense of inadequacy and inferiority and feels unworthy of all that's been given to her.

To disguise her "worthlessness," she commits herself wholeheartedly to looking and acting "perfect." She holds herself to extremely high standards and may work at a fever pitch to earn a string of straight A's. She's unfailingly cooperative and polite, making it a point not to talk back, get angry, act stubborn, or show any negative feelings. She is responsible, hardworking, and exceedingly neat and tidy. But behind this attractive and compliant exterior is a young girl who lives under the tremendous strain of constantly striving for perfection while constantly feeling inferior.

Note: Although girls from upper-class privileged families used to make up the bulk of the anorexic population, they aren't the only victims anymore. It now cuts across class, race, and gender lines.

- *Middle-class female college students (bulimia)*

During the high-stress college years, young women can feel a tremendous pressure to attract men, go on lots of dates, and engage in highly visible social lives. They may also feel that it's absolutely urgent to find that special man, get married, and set up their lives *now* before it's too late. In the extremely competitive singles' market, a high premium is placed on slimness—those who are overweight often find themselves with fewer dates, a lack of marriage opportunities, and diminished social success. To young college-aged women, then, getting and staying thin can take on enormous importance.

- *Male and female athletes engaging in sports that require low body weights*

While only 5 percent of the general population meet the criteria for anorexia and/or bulimia, some experts estimate that from 15 to 62 percent of female athletes exhibit substantially disordered weight-control behaviors.[1] Athletes use weight-loss techniques to improve their performance and/or their appearance, and often find that slimming down brings the desired results. Losing weight can give a wrestler a competitive advantage by putting him into a lower weight class. A slim, lithe body can improve a diver's or figure skater's gracefulness and agility scores. And dropping a few pounds might be able to shave a few seconds off a swimmer's or runner's best time.

By praising athletes for their performance and/or appearance, coaches, teammates, friends, and family can also unintentionally reinforce eating-disordered behaviors. Surprisingly, coaches or older athletes who serve as role models are often the ones who suggest (or hint) that an athlete should try certain dangerous weight-control techniques.[2]

• *Models, actors, and dancers*
Eating disorders are rampant among those whose careers, self-esteem, and identities depend on maintaining the appearance of physical perfection. Actress Sally Field suffered from bulimia for three years during her twenties because she felt that "everybody then was Twiggy except me. I felt immensely unattractive."[3] Janine Turner of television's *Northern Exposure* started modeling at age three and was anorexic by seventeen. She kept her weight at 99 pounds even though, at 5'6", she was 30 pounds underweight. Turner remembers, "If I weighed 100, it would ruin my day."[4] Sandra Dee, a teenage star in the 1960s, began starving herself at age nine. At one point she ate almost nothing but lettuce for an entire year, and twice she overdosed on Epsom salts as a purgative.[5]

In these highly competitive fields, too much weight can kill an otherwise promising career. Those in power (agents, producers, choreographers, advertising agency executives, etc.) exert intense pressure on these young women to conform to unnatural standards of thinness. Especially at risk of developing eating disorders are fash-

ion models and ballet dancers.[6] The average model is
5'9" and weighs about 110 pounds—making her about
24 percent below ideal body weight. Ballet dancers normally carry about 10 percent body fat, which, at half the
recommended amount, is far below the level necessary
to sustain menstruation.

The high-stakes nature of performing arts also exag-
gerates certain personality traits already seen in those
at risk of developing eating disorders. Models, actors,
singers, and the lot typically exhibit a strong desire for
perfection, a high degree of competitiveness, a great
fear of not being good enough, and an unshakable belief in the myth of thinness. What's surprising is *not* that
so many in the performing arts field eventually develop
eating disorders, but that there are actually some people
in this field who *don't*.

- *The sexually abused*

Experts estimate that as many as 70 percent of eating
disorder patients have suffered sexual abuse during
childhood or adolescence.[7] Indeed, one of the many
theories of anorexia is that the victim is starving herself
to keep from developing secondary sex characteristics
("becoming a woman") so that she can ward off further
sexual advances. In some cases, binge eating may also
have its roots in sexual abuse, with the victim eating voraciously to soothe herself or distract herself from unpleasant memories or sensations in her body. She may
also overeat to gain weight so that she'll be less desirable physically and less likely to attract sexual over-
tures. Sexual abuse victims who purge may be using the
act of vomiting as a symbolic way to express rage at the
abuser and to "get rid of the filth" inside.

- *Those with a parent or a sibling who has an
eating disorder*

Eating disorders tend to run in families, although
it's unclear whether the risk increases because of

heredity or through exposure to a similarly disordered environment.

• *Those with a family member who has a mood, anxiety, or substance abuse disorder*
Families of eating-disordered individuals have a high rate of obsessive-compulsive disorders, depression, anxiety, and other mood disorders.[8] Bulimic families are especially likely to have at least one member who abuses alcohol or some other substance.

• *Those with a history of overweight*
Heavy or even slightly heavy people may be more prone to developing eating disorders because 1) they are more likely to make dieting a priority; 2) they are more likely to believe that being thin will solve most of their problems; 3) they may have a disturbed sense of hunger/satiety; and 4) prior dieting may have raised their set points so that nothing short of extreme methods will reduce their weight.

Still, belonging to one or more of the groups listed above doesn't *guarantee* that one will develop an eating disorder—in fact, the vast majority do not. But those who do belong to one or more of these groups should be on guard against disordered eating behaviors. Dieting in particular will be dangerous for them.

Do boys and men get eating disorders too?

Eating disorders do strike men and boys, but males make up only 5 to 10 percent of all eating-disordered patients. Those who are involved in sports or careers that pressure them to maintain a low weight—such as actors, models, jockeys, and gymnasts—are most at risk. Homosexuality can also be a risk factor since slimness is highly valued in the gay community. Research indicates that an estimated 22 percent of male anorexics are homosexual.[9] Another (often overlooked) segment of males with eating disorders are older men who resort to extreme forms of dieting to ward off heart disease. In general, males who develop eating disorders have a history of genuine obesity before onset of the illness.[10] And a good portion of those with Binge Eating Disorder are males (40 percent),[11] making this by far the most common eating disorder affecting men.

What sets an eating disorder in motion?

People with eating disorders are a very diverse group, so there is no single answer to the question.

But are there useful generalizations?

Yes. It seems that eating problems often develop within a young person who has specific psychological issues, lives within a specific family constellation, and lives in a society that values thinness. Anorexics and bulimics are similar in some ways but are, however, quite different in others.

How are anorexics and bulimics similar?

Almost all people with eating disorders have an impaired perception of body shape and size. They tend to be depressed and have mood fluctuations. They tend to think poorly of themselves. They tend to believe that being thin will solve their problems, or conversely that being fat would be horrendous. They have difficulty understanding their own emotions and often express their feelings through food.

How are bulimics different from anorexics?

The most obvious difference is that people with bulimia nervosa tend to be a lot less controlled than people with anorexia. In addition to eating impulsively, people with bulimia are more likely to abuse drugs and engage in destructive sexual experiences. Bulimics tend to get easily frustrated. Neither the anorexic nor the bulimic maintains intimacy very well. While anorexics tend to be somewhat aloof and withdrawn (starving themselves of affection), people with bulimia tend to have more obviously intense relationships. In particular, they tend to get overly attached to someone, get fed up with him, and then feel an overwhelming need to get rid of that person. In a sense, they use bingeing and purging for people as well as for food.

How are anorexics similar to one another?

Most young women with anorexia nervosa were seen as "good girls" when they were little. They were often the kind of children who inspired great pride in their parents and envy in the next-door neighbors. They tended to keep their rooms neat, their hair combed, and their smiles firmly in place. Generally speaking, they don't seem to have problems until after they enter puberty. They may still keep their rooms neat and their hair combed, but they begin to show a steely, inflexible resolve when it comes to food. They may be in outright conflict with their parents, or their weight loss may be kept a secret, but it's a safe bet that there is a war going on. And food is the weapon.

So people with anorexia tend to have a lot of hidden conflict?

When anorexics come into therapy, or when they really open up, we can see the huge paradoxes that characterize their lives. They feel fat but look thin. They feel powerless but are enormously controlling of themselves and the people around them. They may feel totally flawed but appear perfect. They may feel intensely empty and alone while appearing to be popular. They may appear to be special while feeling worthless. They may appear very mature but desperately want to avoid the physical and emotional aspects of adulthood. They might fight intensely with their parents but be unable to separate from them.

How can people feel so different from the way that they appear?

Much of our appearance stems from our psychological defenses. If you feel bad about yourself, for example, you might focus on some aspect of your physical appearance. If you have a tendency to rigid self-discipline and feel bad about yourself, then you might starve yourself into being thin. If you feel worthless, you might do things that make other people think that you're worthwhile. You might even get temporary gratification from the praise. Nevertheless, if you have anorexia, you won't take the praise to heart and will cycle yourself into an exhausting regimen of diet and self-discipline. As can be seen, anorexia is a disorder of eating, but it is also a rather specific psychological problem.

Do anorexics have other psychological problems?

The anorexic is generally sad, distracted, and irritable. These depressive symptoms can begin even before she has lost much weight. If the anorexia progresses to the point of significant weight loss, severe depression is common. And since secrecy and mistrust are common components of anorexia, a person with this disorder generally feels intensely alone.

How would somebody develop anorexia?

There are several overlapping theories about how anorexia develops. Hilde Bruch believed that anorexia developed in girls who didn't have a strong sense of who they were but instead saw themselves as extensions of their parents. This seemed to stem from a mother-daughter interaction in which the mother treated the child according to her own needs rather than the child's needs. Because the little girl never got the opportunity to "swing her elbows" and get her own way, she never developed a strong sense of independence. She was instead forced to rely for her self-esteem on the judgments of others. This would lead her to being an especially good girl. This might also lead to inappropriately harsh self-criticism, since the child never learned that her behavior was acceptable. And it could lead to mistrust, since the girl never felt that she could be open with someone else. And it could lead to black-and-white thinking, since the little girl might not have felt that it was acceptable for her to use her imagination or to play with possibilities. After all, she was supposed to do what her mother told her to do.

Another researcher has added the notion that the anorexic develops a "false self" to guarantee that she won't be abandoned by her mother. Being forced into a rigid, false role of "the good girl" might allow her to stay close to her parents but would also lead to a great deal of resentment. This theory would explain the fear of abandonment in anorexics, a fear that often seems to coexist and alternate with immense, subterranean rage.

There is also a recognizable pattern within some families of anorexics in which different family members become overly enmeshed and the boundaries become blurred between parents and children. This can happen, for example, when there is significant stress in the marriage and one or both of the parents needs the child to act in certain ways, sometimes as a spouse substitute. This can lead the child to feel a premature sense of overresponsibility and a need to overcontrol herself and her environment. It can also be associated with a quest for power and perfection. This can lead to neat bedrooms and well-combed hair. It can also lead to anorexia in a vulnerable person.

In each of these theories, there is considerable emphasis on the family unit's being dysfunctional. It should be made clear, however, that there is rarely one "villain." Instead the family members function as if they were dancing a complex dance, of which they are not fully aware. And because the dance is complex and everyone's participation is required, change in the family system is often sticky.

How does bulimia develop?

Again, nobody knows for sure, and it is different for everybody. Nevertheless, there are some commonly seen patterns in the development of bulimics. First, there appears to be early difficulty with separation, and this is often noticed in both the future bulimic and in the parent. At times the parent can appear to treat the child as an extension of herself. There is often an unusually strong sense of family cohesion, where independence is severely discouraged, and the child does not develop the inner experience of comfortable separations. So far, this sounds a little like the families of anorexics. While the families of anorexics fight, they tend to do so quietly, out of sight of the neighbors; often their fighting consists of an exchange of withholding, rigid glares. The families of bulimics are usually more chaotic, with lots of yelling, screaming, and blaming. Alcoholism, physical abuse, sexual abuse, and neglect are all fairly common in the families of bulimics. Nevertheless, the parents may have a strong need to see themselves as "all good," and the child takes on the "badness" of her family. While she may be quite a good child, the bulimic is generally seen as far more of an impulsive troublemaker than the girl with anorexia. Vomiting can, in a very concrete way, be seen as a way to get rid of "bad" food in the hope of returning herself to a state of "goodness." And if she slips up at all, she is likely to severely condemn herself. It's as if she were a terrible person just because she ate a couple of doughnuts, and if she's bad enough to eat a couple of doughnuts, she might as well eat the whole box. The only hope for salvation is to throw up the "bad" doughnuts, an act that can temporarily return her to "goodness." The major problem with this mode of adaptation is that the person doesn't learn to integrate the bad with the good, which is an important development if the person is to see herself and her world accurately and help prevent the wild gyrations of self-esteem and mood that often underlie the binge-and-purge cycle. This psychological theory, like some of the theories about anorexia, may not make sense at first, but it does often explain the personalities of many people with bulimia.

You talked about psychological characteristics. Do people with anorexia and bulimia have typical ways of thinking?

Again, there is a lot of variability. By definition, though, all anorexics and bulimics misperceive their bodies, and this misperception can verge on the psychotic. They also tend to engage in obsessions and compulsions, often thinking endlessly about food and developing repetitive, ritualistic behaviors. While the obsessions and compulsions generally involve food, they can also spill over into other areas of life, like exercise and schoolwork. There is a tendency to engage in black-and-white thinking and magical thinking. They may see themselves and other people as all good or all bad. They may discount, deflect, or rationalize any comments that interfere with their own distorted belief system. They may overgeneralize, believing, for example that since potatoes are carbohydrates and carbohydrates are fattening, they should avoid all potatoes. These kinds of abnormal thinking are worsened by stress and often kept well hidden and revealed only after considerable therapy.

Are eating disorders genetic?

Not in the way that eye color is genetic. In the case of eating disorders, it seems that people inherit traits and tendencies that may predispose them to developing an eating disorder. Researchers have found, for example, that people with eating disorders tend to have family members with depression, alcoholism, obesity, substance abuse, panic disorder, social phobia, obsessive-compulsive disorder, borderline personality disorder, or post-traumatic stress disorder. Since eating disorders tend to cluster with these other disorders, it does seem that there is a genetic component. In addition, someone would be more likely to develop an eating disorder if she grows up in a family where there are a lot of psychological problems. In this way, eating disorders can be partly "genetic" and partly "environmental."

So the young woman might be primed by a whole set of psychological and family factors. But what makes the behavior start?

Generally speaking, the eating disorder begins in the context of a life change. The change might be going to camp, starting at a new school, going away to college, or getting married. In each of these situations, she is being asked to take on a new level of responsibility or to behave with a maturity that she doesn't yet possess. Perhaps the most common stressful change is puberty. In puberty the young person must confront a whole series of challenges, ranging from becoming adjusted to her developing body to becoming a more sexual being. In the context of losing control of her life, the young woman grabs on to one area that she can control. Food.

What about society's pressure to be thin?

It is hard to overstate the relationship between society's emphasis on thinness and the development of eating disorders. As we've said, anorexia and bulimia didn't exist to any meaningful extent until the past few decades, and it seems clear that eating disorders can grow only in a culture that has a surplus of food and a strong emphasis on physical appearance. It is also clear that the quest for physical perfection takes a toll on many, many people in our society. We are influenced by the media, by coaches, by prospective sexual partners, and by our friends and family, and we often wind up with a distorted sense of beauty. Nevertheless, all of us are exposed to society's obsession with thinness, but only 5 percent of the population develop a problem that officially qualifies as an eating disorder. So there's more to it than just societal pressure.

What role does dieting have in eating disorders?

Unhealthy dieting plays a huge role in the creation and persistence of eating disorders. Both the bulimic and the anorexic tend to starve themselves. For the bulimic, the starvation and hunger eventually become unbearable, and she has to binge, and then she has to purge to make up for her bingeing. The bulimic's "diet" can be seen to lead to overeating and, frequently, weight gain. The anorexic maintains more rigid control over her eating, so she may not gain weight, but she generally becomes obsessed with food. In addition to all the physical and psychological consequences of eating disorders, the quest for the perfect diet leads to exactly the wrong results. In trying to lose weight, the bulimic ends up eating more. In trying to maintain control over her world, the anorexic loses control over what she can eat. Ironically, diets do exactly the opposite of what they're supposed to do. Simply put, any diet that causes you to feel too much hunger is counterproductive.

Chapter Four

THE CYCLE OF CONTROL

The body holds meaning . . . when we probe beneath the surface of our obsession with weight, we will find that a woman obsessed with her body is also obsessed with the limitations of her emotional life. Through her concern with her body, she is expressing a serious concern about the state of her soul.

—Kim Chernin,
  The Obsession: Reflections on the Tyranny of Slenderness

Why would anyone consciously decide to starve herself?

It does seem contrary to nature. Every instinct and natural impulse in our bodies is against it. The all-powerful hunger drive sends signals to our brains and bodies causing pain, weakness, depression, irritability, and aggression that can only be quelled by food. Yet somehow the anorexic is able to eat practically nothing for months or even years.

In the same vein, the bulimic not only starves herself but uses food as a weapon to perpetrate physical violence on her body.

Whether anorexic or bulimic, the eating-disordered person quickly becomes exhausted, depressed, and trapped by what she's doing—yet for some reason she continues her destructive behavior. Why? *Because controlling her food intake has become a metaphor for controlling her life.* The truth is, eating disorders are not really about food or weight—they are about a "disordered sense of self."

How does a "disordered sense of self" bring on an eating disorder?

The origins of an eating disorder often date back to childhood, when a girl's emotional or physical needs weren't properly recognized or responded to. For example, when she was a baby and she cried, her parents may not have comforted or soothed her often enough or soon enough. This can create a deficiency in her ability to self-soothe as she gets older. An older child who complains that she's tired or hungry and is angrily told, "You're so selfish!" may learn to ignore her internal cures and begin to doubt her worth.

When a child's emotional or physical needs are met with abuse, ridicule, or a lack of interest or validation too many times, she may learn that repressing or denying these needs is a "safer" way to go. But this seriously jeopardizes her ability to develop a cohesive personality and to feel that she is a valid, worthwhile person. Her self-esteem drops. Her personality development is derailed as she forms a distorted self-image ("I'm bad; I'm stupid; I'm self-centered") or no self-image at all ("I'm invisible; I'm undeserving; I don't know what I want"). Without a positive self-image, she'll have an extremely hard time functioning in an adult world. Like a ship without ballast, she will have nothing to keep her firmly centered and stabilized.

Food, diets, and weight loss, then, may actually take the place of a loving caretaker in her life. They can be used to make her feel safe, secure, and whole. On the most basic level, food may be equated with love, diets and eating rituals with structure and control, and weight loss with success and validation. But it gets much more complex than that. Amazingly, an eating disorder can provide a whole host of coping functions.

What coping functions can an eating disorder provide?

The eating disorder can fulfill underlying emotional needs that are not being satisfied in other, more positive ways. For example:

Fasting or rigid dieting may provide:

• *A way to "purify" the self*—Long used by saints and members of religious societies, fasting is employed as a method of denying or stamping out human feelings (such as pain, hunger, or fatigue) to prove that one is truly one's own master. Fasting or rigid dieting may be a way for the eating-disordered individual to maintain her self-esteem and/or prove her "worthiness."

• *Structure, control, identity*—In an otherwise chaotic world, the diet (or fast) may be the one thing the individual feels she can rely on as a constant. The rules are absolutely clear and concrete, bringing clear, concrete results. If she follows them to the letter, she can then claim her reward—that of being "good," "thin," and "in control."

> "Weird as it may sound, starving made me feel strong. It was something that was mine alone; nobody could do anything about it but me. As long as the hunger pangs were booming, I knew I was all right."
>
> —Daria,
> seventeen-year-old anorexic

• *Protection from sexuality or sexual abuse*—A person who has been sexually abused or who fears sexuality may use dieting as a way to keep or regain her childlike body. She may gladly exchange her womanly curves for a child's straight-up-and-down figure, which she feels is "safer."

Bingeing may provide:

• *Protection against sexuality or sexual abuse*—Another way of "dealing with" sexual abuse or fear of sexuality is *gaining* weight. Getting fat, the individual may believe, will make her either unattractive enough to discourage sexual advances or big enough to fight off her abuser.

• *Comfort, solace, nurturance*—In an unloving, hostile, or indifferent world, food may temporarily supply the warm, contented, cared-for feelings that are missing in real life. Food makes the individual feel good, especially when she feels bad.

• *Calming, relief from tension, distraction*—Most of the eating disordered suffer from high levels of anxiety. When they "let go" and binge, they experience relief and escape from their problems, if only temporarily. This instant gratification can encourage a person to binge in response to emotional upsets rather than deal with the upsets directly. For example, a bulimic may say, "When I heard that my sister got engaged, I was so depressed I went home and ate everything in the refrigerator." Or "I was so mad at my boyfriend that I had to do something, so I bought a big chocolate cake and ate the whole thing."

"For me, dieting was like living in a pressure cooker. I'd be so good, counting every calorie, watching every mouthful, but as the days went by I'd get tenser and tenser until finally I couldn't stand it. I'd go home one night and eat a couple of loaves of bread, an entire jar of peanut butter and a big jug of jam, leftover casseroles, and anything else I could find. Afterward I'd be exhausted and sick, but the tension would be gone."

—Doris,
forty-five-year-old binge eater

Purging may provide:

• *A way to release anger*—The act of vomiting may be a metaphor for spitting out angry feelings that are bottled up inside. The individual's lack of power, self-esteem, or positive self-image may make it impossible for her to express her angry feelings directly, so instead she lets it all out by vomiting. That this involves self-inflicted violence (i.e., fingers down the throat) may also serve a purpose by helping to assuage some of the guilt she feels. Strange as it seems, she may feel that she doesn't have a right to get angry or that it's her fault that she's been victimized.

> "For years my mother would call me every single day, and I had to talk to her or she'd get me on the phone at another time and yell at me. She's always been so difficult and demanding, and years ago I learned not to 'talk back' or try to stand up for myself. It was so much easier just to go along with her.
>
> "But about a year ago I started throwing up right after her phone calls, and for some weird reason that made me feel better. After a while it didn't even matter if I had anything in my stomach or not. If I didn't, I'd go drink a glass of water after I hung up. *Then* I'd throw up. It was just something I had to do."
>
> —Gerianne,
> twenty-six-year-old bulimic

• *A means of self-punishment*—Some individuals become so furious with themselves for bingeing that they induce vomiting or take laxatives strictly for their unpleasant physical effects. Some bulimics also cut themselves. They generally do this not in an effort to kill themselves but as a way to feel less numb or to gain control over terrible feelings. In many ways, purging can function much like this superficial cutting.

"I'm always so disgusted with myself after a binge. I just can't believe that I keep doing it! And each time, I say to myself afterward, 'Okay, you fat pig, now you have to bring *all* of that food back up again.' I make myself drink a lot of water, and I keep throwing up until I'm sure I've 'paid my dues.' "

—Janet,
twenty-one-year-old bulimic

• *Gratification, relaxation, a "high"*—Not only can purging immediately release the guilty, anxious, fearful feelings that follow a binge, it can have a profound effect on the brain. The act of purging can trigger the release of certain brain chemicals that bring about a feeling of well-being, relief, and relaxation. Some have even described the effects as "orgasmic."

Bulimics can and often do get hooked on the "high" associated with purging. Over time, the act of purging, which started out as a way to compensate for bingeing, can become a way to relieve anxiety instead. It's not uncommon for a bulimic to binge strictly as a means of inducing a purge—it's the purge and the good feelings that accompany it that she really wants.

Starving, bingeing, or purging may provide:

• *Protection from intimacy*—With her self-development and image formation disrupted, the individual is likely to have problems relating to others. Practicing an eating disorder, then, which requires spending plenty of time alone, can become a convenient excuse for her to withdraw. Increased isolation may appeal to her because it seems less painful. However, it will make her condition even worse as she becomes more and more self-absorbed and less in touch with reality.

• *A way to get help*—A desperate individual may feel that she won't be taken seriously unless she does something drastic. An anorexic may drop to an alarmingly low weight to make others "prove" that they love her. A bulimic may leave empty food cartons or boxes of laxatives lying around in plain sight, cupboards completely bare, or vomitus on the toilet seat or counters. Because she is unable to ask for help, these indirect methods may be her only communication tools.

"When I starved myself down to 70 pounds, they finally had to sit up and take notice."

—Jamie,
fifteen-year-old anorexic

• *A way to get attention and protection from her parents without being pressured*—By becoming an "invalid," she may be able to gain or regain the status of a loved and cherished child—*without* the pressure to perform. This may be reason enough to make some anorexics reluctant to give up the disease (their "power"). "If I get well," she might say, "they won't pay attention to me anymore." Unfortunately, this thinking encourages her dependence on others, one of the very things that brought the illness on.

"What becomes clear during extensive contact is that these youngsters had come to an impasse in their lives: to continue as before had become impossible. . . . Their own bodies became the arena for their only exercise of control."

—Hilde Bruch, M.D.,
The Golden Cage: The Enigma of Anorexia Nervosa

Do all eating disorders begin with a diet?

Although some eating disorders may grow directly out of conflict or anger or a need for control, most begin with intentionally restricted eating. Over time, this restricted eating can and does make an eating disorder even worse by:

- *interfering with the body's ability to signal hunger and satiety (fullness);*
- *promoting obsessive thoughts about food and eating;*
- *encouraging black-and-white thinking;*
- *encouraging rigid, overly controlled behavior;*
- *triggering bingeing;*
- *setting the dieter up for failure, which can lead to more desperate weight-loss measures.*

How does dieting interfere with hunger and satiety signals?

We are all born "knowing" how much we need to eat. Even a newborn baby can tell you plainly when she needs to be "refueled" and when she's had enough. Unfortunately, dieting can cause us to "unlearn" what we knew at birth, making it possible for us to stuff ourselves with too much food or starve ourselves to the point of death. Dieting encourages this "unlearning" in the following ways:

- *The diet dictates when and what to eat; hunger and satiety become irrelevant*—Anyone who's ever been on a diet can tell you that to follow it successfully you'll have to learn to ignore your body's hunger and satiety signals. The diet dictates what, when, and how much you can eat. How the dieter *feels* at any given time is completely irrelevant. She'll find herself thinking, "I'm starving, but I have to wait another hour before I can eat." Or "I guess I'd better eat all of this now, even though I'm full, or I'll be hungry later." Eventually she can become so out of touch with her body's signals that she can't tell when she's hungry and when she's not.

• *Dieting interrupts normal hunger and satiety signals*—Confusion about hunger and satiety is a common problem for both anorexics and bulimics. The anorexic may feel "stuffed" after eating two crackers, while the bulimic doesn't feel full even though she's just eaten a half gallon of ice cream, an entire chicken, and a dozen cupcakes!

There are physiological reasons for both of these phenomena that can be traced directly to dieting. For example, the chronic starving of the anorexic causes the stomach to slow its emptying rate so it can absorb food as efficiently as possible. Eventually even a small meal can make this sluggish stomach feel unpleasantly full. The bulimic, on the other hand, may be able to eat tremendous quantities of food because dieting has changed the level of certain chemicals in her brain. She no longer receives the proper signals telling her when she's had enough.

• *Dieting makes a person more likely to binge*—The body is "hardwired" to protect itself against starvation. During times of famine (or dieting), the body automatically slows down its basal metabolic rate to conserve calories. At the same time, it increases hunger by releasing greater amounts of insulin, hoping to encourage its owner to eat. Many bulimics start to release insulin into their bloodstreams whenever they see, smell, or even think about food![1] Insulin lowers the blood sugar, causing hunger and a craving for sweets. The craving can be so intense that once the individual finally starts to eat, she can continue far past the point of healthy satisfaction. Her hunger will be maintained even after her stomach has had its fill.

The correlation between dieting and binge eating has been shown in many studies, but probably the most dramatic results were obtained in an experiment done by Keys et al. in 1950.[2] Thirty-six young, healthy, psychologically normal males were recruited for a year-long experiment on the effects of starvation. For the first three months they ate normally, for the next six months they were given only half as much food, and during the final three months they were gradually re-fed. After six months of semistarvation, when the men were allowed to eat normally again, they "ate more or less continuously" and reported an *increase* of hunger immediately *after* their meals. Some men engaged in binges of between 8,000 and 10,000 calories a day; others stuffed themselves to the point of being sick and still didn't feel satisfied. Five months after the end of the experiment, most men had finally normalized their eating patterns, but some continued "extreme overconsumption."

Bingeing actually makes good sense when it comes to survival—after a period of famine, a starving animal needs to stock up while the food supply is good. It follows that when the modern-day dieter imposes semi-starvation conditions on herself (by going on a diet), her body will naturally want to binge to make up for the deficit. She'll find herself wanting to eat like crazy as her body fights to defend its natural weight, and she'll stay hungry even after eating *the same amount of food* that would have satisfied her before. This phenomenon is *not* limited to bulimics or binge eaters. Normal, average people will experience it if semistarvation goes on long enough. And fully 50 percent of anorexics eventually become bingers when their bodies revolt against their rigid, restrictive diets.

• *Just the act of dieting makes a person more likely to overeat*—There is some evidence that dieters, as a group, react differently to food than nondieters, no matter what their weight.

In one experiment, a group of dieters and a group of nondieters were each given high-calorie milk shakes and then asked to do taste tests on several other foods. When it came time to do the taste testing, the nondieters automatically ate smaller amounts of the foods than they would have if they hadn't had the milkshakes. But the dieters actually ate *larger* amounts of the foods after having their milkshakes. The difference: The nondieters responded to physical cues, eating according to their hunger and satiety signals. The dieters, on the other hand, responded to psychological cues. Once they had eaten something they thought was "high calorie," they *stopped resisting the urge to eat* and ate more than they would have if they hadn't had the high-calorie drink. ("Oh, well, now that I've blown it I might as well eat.")

When the experiment was repeated with a drink that was actually very low in calories but that the dieters *believed* was high calorie, they also ate more. This confirmed that the amount of food the dieters ate depended on their psychological states.[3]

How does dieting affect a person psychologically?

Once the dieter's body gets the signal that the food supply is too low, or that she's dropped to a lower-than-natural weight, strange things can begin to happen to her psychologically. She may find herself constantly thinking about food. She may spend all her free time clipping out recipes, planning menus, or cooking elaborate dishes that she pushes on others (without eating any herself). She might even start dreaming about food at night. And no wonder—her body is hungry!

If the diet goes on for more than a few days, she'll probably get depressed, her self-esteem will drop, and she'll find herself wanting to spend more and more time alone. Unfortunately, isolation is probably the worst thing for her because it will keep her away from the people and situations that might stabilize her. As depression and isolation increase, food becomes more and more of an obsession. Finally, her body's urge for food may become so strong that she binges, eating far greater amounts of food than she would ever have dreamed of eating before she started dieting.

These mental and emotional changes are the direct result of dieting. You don't have to have an eating disorder to experience them. In the Keys starvation experiment mentioned earlier, healthy, psychologically normal men became preoccupied with food, talking, reading, and daydreaming about it constantly. Many began reading cookbooks and collecting recipes. Much time was spent planning how the day's allotment of food would be eaten, and many dawdled over their food for hours to "make it last." As semistarvation continued, they grew anxious, irritable, depressed, and prone to angry outbursts. Over time they became more withdrawn and isolated, claiming that it was "too tiring" to have contact with others, and most experienced periods of severe emotional distress. All these changes were wrought by the extreme restriction of food.

Once an eating disorder is triggered, what keeps it going?

A whole series of psychological factors feed into each other to keep an eating disorder "in business." In his book *The Deadly Diet*, Terence Sandbek refers to this process as the Control Cycle."[4] The cycle begins when an individual feels that her life is out of control and focuses on her weight and eating habits as both the cause of and the solution to her problems. While attempting to regain power by controlling her weight, she gets caught up in a vicious cycle that leaves her feeling even more powerless than before.

There are five parts to the Control Cycle, each triggering the next and perpetuating the cycle.[5] The cycle begins with *environmental triggers*, which lead to *destructive thinking*, which triggers *stress*, which prompts *ineffective coping behaviors*, which encourage *destructive emotions*, making *environmental triggers* even more inflammatory and causing greater amounts of *destructive thinking*. The cycle then repeats itself, becoming stronger and more destructive over time, and soon any of its elements can set off any of the others. (As you can see in the diagram below, arrows originate from each element, indicating that each element can set off any or all of the other elements.)

THE CONTROL CYCLE

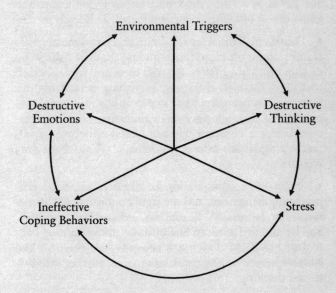

How does the Control Cycle work?

• *Environmental triggers*—We begin with an individual who desperately wants to gain control of her eating habits and her weight—often a metaphor for gaining control of her life. Psychological, familial, and physiological factors make her a prime target for eating disorders. Then something in her environment sets off a chain reaction, like tipping over the first domino in a long line. It could be an unflattering picture of herself, a new bulge she notices when looking in the mirror, or a comment someone makes about her "chubbiness." It can also be a positive comment ("Oh, you've lost weight. You look great!") or a date with someone she really likes. Whatever the impetus, the environmental trigger plays into her feelings of inferiority, her fear of what others think of her, and her desperate need to appear "perfect." She develops a fierce determination to go on a diet and gain control of her life once and for all. This leads to:

• *Destructive thinking*—Like a cruel taskmaster, she clamps down on herself, demanding that she "shape up or ship out." She makes up strict diets and forces herself to follow them to the letter, punishing herself for not living up to her own high expectations. She may also put herself through rigorous, exhausting bouts of exercise. Under a constant barrage of self-criticism, her already fragile self-esteem plummets. These behaviors trigger:

• *Stress*—The combination of negative self-talk, self-punishing behaviors, and the rigid conditions of the diet results in depression, headaches, exhaustion, insomnia, and heightened anxiety. She obsesses about gaining control of her body, which has become "the enemy," and isolates herself as she continues to sink further into distorted thinking. This prompts:

• *Ineffective coping behaviors*—Her chosen method of coping will determine the kind of eating disorder she develops. She may respond to the stress by restricting her food intake even further, becoming anorexic. She could start bingeing (but not purging) and develop Binge Eating Disorder. She might binge and purge, becoming bulimic. Or she could engage in a combination of any of these behaviors. The one thing that all of these coping mechanisms have in common is that they encourage:

• *Destructive emotions*—Ineffective coping behaviors commonly lead to guilt, depression, self-hatred, anxiety, and fear. These feelings greatly increase the low self-esteem, worry, and out-of-control feelings that started the cycle in the first place. She feels worse than she did when she began, and more desperate than ever to lose that dreaded weight. Her thoughts become even more destructive, triggering greater stress, which exacerbates the environmental triggers or leads directly to further use of ineffective coping strategies. The Cycle of Control has her firmly in its destructive grasp.

How does the Cycle of Control work in anorexia?

As an example, let's look at Lisa, a twenty-two-year-old graduate student who has been anorexic for four years. The only child of working-class parents, Lisa had essentially lived her life as a little girl until she was eighteen. Unsure of her worth (she'd often heard how much her father had wanted a boy), she had maintained her place in the family by conforming in an exaggerated way. She worked hard to be the perfect daughter, never talking back, studying hard, doing her utmost to win the approval of her parents. As she would later say, "I made *sure* they would love me. I was always so good, they just couldn't help it."

At the age of eighteen, when Lisa went away to college in another state, she began to show signs of anorexia. This new phase of independence served as the *environmental trigger* for her illness. At college, Lisa discovered that her compulsive "good girl" attitude didn't exactly ingratiate her with her fellow students. She found herself at a real disadvantage because she had no concept of who she was or what she wanted. (Her parents had always provided her with those answers.) She needed a much stronger sense of self and a more assertive, mature, independent way of dealing with the world. She puts it this way: "All the things that were right when I was at home (being good, following the rules, not questioning authority, etc.) were suddenly not right once I got out on my own. I was completely unprepared. I didn't know how to *be* anymore. I ended up just staying in my room, studying and worrying about getting fat."

Deciding that she needed to lose ten pounds, Lisa began dieting. As the pounds started to melt away, she was buoyed by the attention and praise she got from her fellow students. She had finally found something she was really good at, something that brought her admiration. But as more weight dropped off, Lisa plunged into the *destructive thinking* phase.

Depression, restlessness, and irritability—all psychological symptoms of her semistarved state—began to plague her. She didn't feel like being around others, so she spent most of her time in her room reading recipes and inspecting her emaciated body. The dieting, destructive thinking, isolation, and extremely high standards that she set for herself greatly increased the *stress* in her life.

To compensate, Lisa adopted several *ineffective coping behaviors*. Feeling superior to others when she ate little or nothing, she learned to eat very, very slowly, "brainwashing" herself to believe that she was full after only a few bites. She'd avoid eating for as long as she could, then ward it off just a *little* bit longer—until another hour, another meal, or better yet another day had passed. She also found that she could eat "vicariously." When she went home to visit her parents, she would plan and cook gourmet meals for them. Then she would watch them eat, insisting that they finish every bite, while she ate nothing. She used a variety of excuses, including: "I ate too much while cooking," "My stomach is upset today," or "I'll eat later when I get hungry."

As the illness wore on, Lisa became more self-absorbed, more isolated, more caught up in her obsessions. Often up half the night doing calisthenics, she would rise every morning promptly at 6:00 A.M. to run ten miles. She also swam fifty laps and took two high-impact aerobic classes daily. "I just had to do it," she says. "There was this demon inside me that forced me to keep pushing, pushing, pushing. I felt like something terrible would happen if I ever stopped." By now eating made her so nervous and angry with herself that she could barely get anything down. Her daily diet consisted of lettuce leaves, iced tea, and an occasional can of tomato juice.

When she did eat a cracker or a piece of bread, or neglect to do a full hour of jogging, her anxiety levels soared. She mercilessly "beat herself up" with *destructive emotions* like self-hatred, anger turned inward, and depression. If she couldn't exercise absolute dominance over her body, she felt utterly worthless. This *destructive thinking* led to even more *stress* and *ineffective coping behaviors*, causing the Cycle of Control to be repeated over and over again.

How does the Cycle of Control work in bulimia?

Mary Jo was born out of wedlock to Sarah, a nineteen-year-old high school dropout who lived with her aging, old-fashioned parents in a small town in the Midwest. Mary Jo's grandparents knew that Sarah was much too wild and irresponsible to be a good mother, so they adopted Mary Jo themselves, pretending that she was a change-of-life baby.

Although less than exciting, Mary Jo's elderly "parents" loved her and provided her with a good, solid foundation. They never did get around to telling her the circumstances surrounding her birth. "Why bring it up?" they said to each other. "Maybe no one will ever find out." In the meantime, Sarah got married, moved away, and had a few children of her own. Mary Jo and her "parents" didn't see much of Sarah through the years, but word got back to them that both she and her husband were alcoholic and that their children were not well cared for.

Disaster struck when Mary Jo was eight years old. Her "mother" died suddenly of a stroke, and just a week later her "father" followed with a fatal heart attack. Suddenly Sarah, whom she had seen only a few times, appeared out of the blue with the news that *she* was really Mary Jo's mother and that Mary Jo was to come and live with her now.

Thus began a nightmarish period in Mary Jo's life as she was plunged into a chaotic family life that included alcoholism, drug abuse, hostility, and severe criticism. She had to learn to cook, clean, and take care of her younger brothers and sisters while enduring endless blame, criticism, and physical abuse. To make matters worse, once Mary Jo turned thirteen, her stepfather began paying nightly visits to her bedroom. As soon as that happened (*environmental trigger*), Mary Jo stopped eating.

"I really wanted to go back and be eight years old again," she says. "I began to think that if I could just get back my old body, I could somehow get back my old life. And besides, *he* didn't used to bother me when I was smaller."

Seeing her newly emerging curves as a symbol of her new, hated life, Mary Jo dieted with a vengeance to get rid of them, coupling the diet with *destructive thinking*. "I hated myself for every single bite of food I took. I was convinced that thinness was my only way out and that eating just contributed to my problems." For two weeks she existed on a daily diet of two pieces of bread, a half cup of cottage cheese, and one pear.

By the end of the two weeks, Mary Jo had progressed to the *stress* stage, having become hideously depressed, exhausted, and so nervous she could hardly sleep. Her *ineffective coping behavior* emerged as a binge, which led to a purge. "My nerves were stretched as tight as a rubber band. Finally, I got up in the middle of the night, went into the kitchen, and started eating. I don't even know what I ate, but I do know that there was no food left in the morning. Afterward I felt really panicky because I knew I was going to get fat, right when it was so important to get skinny. I'd heard that some people put their fingers down their throat to make themselves throw up, so I tried it. It was such a relief to get rid of it all! But then I felt like such a disgusting, worthless person." These *destructive emotions* led to *destructive thinking* as she clamped down on herself, resolving to get right back on the diet and do it right this time. "I had to get thin; I had to get control of myself. I decided to be extra strict with myself the next day."

When her parents discovered that she'd eaten all of the family's food, Mary Jo got a beating. "That was okay, because I knew I deserved it. But the weirdest thing was, I felt like doing it all over again the next night. I managed to put it off for a whole week. Then one day, when I found my mom passed out on the floor from drinking, I thought, 'I don't care. I'm gonna eat whatever I want!'"

The *stress* of Mary Jo's family situation, coupled with her *destructive thinking*, made her desperate for self-soothing and relief from the anxiety. She used *ineffective coping behaviors* to handle the stress. That night she stole a ten-dollar bill from her stepfather's wallet and went to a local convenience store, where she spent the whole thing on candy bars and two huge bottles of soda. Then she went out in the back alley, stuffed it all down, and immediately threw it up into a Dumpster. Her *destructive emotions* were evident right away.

"Afterward I felt like an old dishrag—I knew I was a disgusting pig. But at least I didn't feel so nervous and keyed up anymore. After that I still kept on dieting, but whenever I started feeling too bad or nervous, I'd go buy a bunch of candy bars and do my thing. It was my way of making myself feel better." Mary Jo's Cycle of Control continued for ten years.

How do you break the cycle?

If you've found yourself caught in the Cycle of Control, don't make the mistake of believing that you'll somehow grow out of it or that you can figure out how to stop on your own. Once it's begun, eating-disordered behavior can be extremely difficult to stop, and the longer it goes on, the harder stopping it becomes. Eating disorders are deadly—but luckily they are also treatable, especially if they're caught early. *It is imperative that you get treatment as soon as you can from professionals who are specially trained to handle eating disorders.* The sooner you get help, the sooner you will be on your way to a healthier, happier life.

In the next chapter we'll explain what "getting help" means—including which professionals are best qualified to treat eating disorders, what they do, how to find them, and how to tell when hospitalization is necessary.

Chapter Five

TREATMENT FOR EATING DISORDERS

I shall gather myself into myself again,
I shall take my scattered selves and make them one. . .
—Sara Teasdale

I think I have an eating disorder and I really want to get rid of it. What do I do now?

Congratulations! The moment that you decided to change your behavior, your treatment began. Now it's time to relax, take some deep breaths, and mull over the possibilities. Believe it or not, your eating disorder serves an important function in your life. While it often feels horrendous, it may also feel like the only thing you've got. Allow yourself some comfort as you develop a treatment plan. Maybe now is the time to tell your gynecologist that you haven't had a period in six months and you think you might be anorexic. Maybe you are already in psychotherapy but have neglected to mention that you vomit every day—better let your psychotherapist know now, before any more time goes by. Maybe now is the time to go to the library and get some books on the subject while learning relaxation techniques from a massage therapist or a yoga class. The possibilities are many, but you should start with something. And when you're ready to get serious about solving your eating problems, you'll need to see certain professionals who are qualified to help you do just that.

Everyone is unique, and your treatment must be carefully designed to fit who you are. For example, you may engage in only occasional bingeing and purging. You may be able to read this book and recognize that your bulimia is a direct result of a fad diet. You may be able to regain normal eating habits very quickly and then watch the binge-and-purge cycle just fade away. But most people need more help than this.

My mother says I don't have any time, that I have to see somebody right away. Is she overreacting?

That's hard to know. If uncontrolled, eating disorders can be life threatening. If you weigh less than 70 percent of your expected weight, you may well be in serious physical danger. You need to see a physician urgently. Similarly, if you are suicidal, you need to consult with a psychiatrist as soon as possible. In both situations, hospitalization may be necessary. At the same time, many specialists in eating disorders can work effectively with outpatients who are at very low weights and/or have occasional suicidal thoughts. The important issue here is that your treatment needs to be customized for you, especially if your behavior is threatening your life. You will need to come up with some sort of treatment program.

**What kinds of things are included
in a treatment program?**

All people with eating disorders need to address medical, psychological, and nutritional issues. As stated earlier, however, *eating disorders* is such a broad term, and people are so variable, that there is no single treatment program that will work for everybody. For example, an anorexic might see her physician first, especially if her physical problems are severe. Her physician might then refer her to a therapist and a dietitian. Another person might see a therapist first and then go to a general medical doctor and then a dietitian.

Since several issues need to be addressed, many people decide to go to an eating disorders clinic. One of the real advantages to a specialized clinic is that people within the clinic are experienced in coordinating the actions of different members of the treatment team. This is an especially important issue for people with eating disorders. Too often, different aspects of the patient's life get lost in the shuffle. This is partly because of the complexity of some eating disorders but also because people with eating disorders tend to be quite secretive. Such programs are not available everywhere, however, and they may not feel right to you. There are other options.

Assembling your own treatment team is a more common alternative to hospitalization or going to a specialized clinic. To do this, you should try to see several specialists who will be willing to talk to one another during the course of your treatment. You will almost certainly need to see a general medical doctor. Eating disorders are often accompanied by treatable medical problems, but you will need to tell your doctor about your eating habits so that he or she will know what to look for. Becoming more open about your behavior is an important part of your treatment, so make use of this opportunity. You will need to learn more about basic nutrition, and it is therefore important that you consider getting a consultation with a registered dietitian. Finally, the cornerstone of most treatments is psychological counseling. Each of these issues will be discussed.

Do I really need to see my internist?

Your physical problems may be minimal at this point, but it's still a good idea to get a general physical exam and some lab work. It may not be easy for you to expose your behavior and your body to a doctor. Try.

What would my physician be looking for?

Your doctor will probably begin by weighing you and taking a history of your dieting and eating behavior. Then he or she will perform a physical examination, looking in particular for any problems associated with starving, bingeing, purging, or the abuse of medications.

If you have experienced significant weight loss, your doctor might look for low blood pressure, a slow heartbeat, cold intolerance, swelling of the hands and feet, and the growth of a baby-fine hair on your body. Your abdomen might be bloated, which is related to constipation and delayed emptying of the stomach. You might have stopped having your menstrual period. You will probably be depressed and irritable. You may have an abnormal sensation of taste. Laboratory tests might reveal reduced thyroid metabolism; a loss of heart muscle with changes in your electrocardiogram (ECG); high cholesterol; and a lowered white blood cell count, which makes you less able to fight off infection.

If you purge by vomiting or abusing laxatives, your doctor might find inflammation and enlargement of the salivary glands, which leads to "chipmunk cheeks." Your stomach and esophagus may have developed ulcers. Your bowels might have become dysfunctional. Your teeth might be decayed. You might have developed seizures. Laboratory tests could show electrolyte abnormalities, especially low chloride, magnesium, and potassium levels. These abnormalities are generally treatable and usually resolve themselves once the starvation and/or purging have stopped.

You said I might need to see a dietitian. I know everything there is to know about diets. Why should I waste my time?

Some people with eating disorders are experts at certain aspects of nutrition. For example, you might know calorie counts with startling accuracy. Nevertheless, it is very likely that you have some big misconceptions about food and its role in weight gain and loss. These misconceptions can drive your eating disorder and make you miserable. A dietitian can help you learn about food, weight gain and loss, and the creation of a normal eating pattern. The dietitian's work is part of the process that leads to a healthy attitude toward food.

So a dietitian acts like a teacher?

Education is an important part of the dietitian's role. She can help you learn about your body and how it handles food. She can teach you about the physiological effects of starvation, bingeing, and purging. She can describe the components of a good, balanced diet. She can address facts and fallacies about food and answer your questions.

A dietitian may do more, however, than just educate you about facts. As part of the ongoing treatment, your dietitian can help you normalize your own eating habits and your own reactions to eating. One of her goals will be to teach you to eat regular, well-balanced meals, a habit that should decrease or eliminate your urge to fast, binge, and purge. She can help you recognize that your eating habits are related to psychological issues. She can support you as your weight fluctuates in response to your new eating habits. And she can help you maintain an appropriate weight without resorting to unhealthy or destructive behaviors.

How do you choose a dietitian?

Although many people use the words *dietitian* and *nutritionist* interchangeably, it's important to remember that anyone can call herself a nutritionist. There is no legal definition of *nutritionist*, and there is no education and no license required for that title. A registered dietitian (R.D.), however, has been extensively trained in nutrition, food, and the biochemistry of the body; holds at least a bachelor's degree from an accredited college or university; and has completed a hospital internship. She may have received a master's degree.

Since the psychological issues are so entwined with the food issues in eating disorders, it may be important to find a dietitian who is trained in psychotherapeutic counseling (sometimes referred to as a nutrition therapists). These dietitians often work as part of the team in eating disorder treatment programs, or they may see patients privately.

To find a dietitian or a nutrition therapist, you may want to ask your doctor, psychologist, or psychiatrist for a referral. You can also call your local hospital, consult the yellow pages, or call the American Dietetic Association at (800) 366-1655. You may want to interview more than one dietitian before beginning your work.

What should I know about my dietitian?

As part of the initial phase of your work with the dietitian, you should learn how much the sessions cost, how long they last, the recommended frequency, and whether your insurance will cover some or all of the cost. You should find out if you are expected to pay for missed sessions and whether she is available for telephone sessions. If you are anorexic, you should find out whether she plans to weigh you; if you are bulimic, weighing is probably not necessary. You should work with her in deciding the nature of treatment and the goals for treatment.

What kinds of things will my dietitian ask me?

The initial sessions will probably be devoted to obtaining a careful history of your eating patterns and your weight. She will want to know when your eating disorder began and what in particular "triggers" your disorder. For example, you might redouble your starvation efforts when you are faced with a work deadline; the deadline is a "trigger" for your disorder. You might work with the dietitian to lessen the impact of these triggers. If applicable, she will explore the details of your bingeing and purging. She will ask about your goals for therapy. In general, the evaluation phase is devoted to determining the nature of your eating disorder and the best path for your recovery.

What does the dietitian do after the evaluation is over?

That depends on the evaluation. For most people, education is important. People with eating disorders are especially prone to food fads and misinformation. For example, Jeanette, a twenty-four-year-old bulimic, knew that bananas had more calories than most other fruits. Therefore, in her mind, bananas were "fattening"; they were on her list of "bad foods." She scrupulously avoided eating bananas or anything that contained them, and if she accidentally ended up eating even a small portion of one, she instantly felt anxious, guilty, and desperate to purge. Jeanette's dietitian might point out that there are no "good" or "bad" foods. All foods contain calories; weight gain depends on how much a person eats, not the fact that a certain "bad" food has touched her lips. Bananas, for instance, have no magical properties that instantly cause weight gain. In fact, half a banana is no more "fattening" than a small apple or one piece of dry bread, since they all have the same number of calories. One goal of the treatment would be to help Jeanette understand her misconception, gradually adding bananas to her diet, while helping her deal with the anxiety aroused by eating the forbidden fruit.

Will the dietitian force me to eat a lot of food?

The dietitian will gradually reintroduce you to "normal" eating. She'll probably begin by working with you to set up a meal plan that includes foods you like and are used to eating. You'll start by eating meals that aren't much bigger than what you've currently been eating, but you *will* begin to eat on a regular basis (breakfast, lunch, dinner, and possibly a few snacks). In addition, each meal will include healthy foods containing protein, carbohydrates, and fat. In time, you'll learn that eating the occasional doughnut or french fry is not the end of the world.

As you get used to eating normal portions at regular intervals, your body will begin to regulate itself. Your desire to binge should lessen, or even go away, as you stop starving yourself. Depression and anxiety usually improve. You will probably feel more energetic and mentally focused.

Where does psychotherapy come in?

Psychotherapy (talk therapy) is the cornerstone of most eating disorder treatments. This is most often done on a one-to-one basis with a therapist. You and your therapist might do cognitive-behavioral therapy or you might do a more interpersonal, psychological therapy, or you might do some combination. You might also be helped by family therapy, couples therapy, group therapy, or a support group. Medications might be useful. There are lots of choices, and we will talk about each of them.

What should I do first?

Generally, it's a good idea to focus first on the most pressing issue. If you have a serious problem with drugs and a mild case of bulimia, for example, you should probably get treatment first for the drug problem. Similarly, if you have a serious depression, most therapists would probably try to treat the depression immediately. Talk over your needs and goals with your therapist.

How should I choose a therapist?

Choose a therapist who feels trustworthy. He or she should have experience and expertise in the field of eating disorders and should seem genuinely interested in your problems. At first the most important aspect of therapy is to gain trust in each other. Then when the going gets rough, you will have a relationship that can withstand some conflict.

Should I pick a psychiatrist or psychologist or social worker or analyst? What's the difference?

The selection is based mainly on personal preference. We will outline the ways that therapists differ, but your successful recovery is based on how well you work with the therapist, not on the nature of his or her graduate degree.

You should be aware that psychiatrists have gone to medical school and have then done at least four years of specialty training in psychiatry. As physicians, psychiatrists are the only therapists who can prescribe medications, which are often useful to people with eating disorders. If you might need hospitalization, you should know that psychiatrists generally control hospital admissions. Psychiatrists tend to be the most expensive kind of therapist, though most insurance plans cover some or most of the cost. Some psychiatrists do psychotherapy all day. Others do little therapy but a lot of medication treatments. You might see a medicating psychiatrist if your primary therapist is a social worker or psychologist.

Psychologists have earned either a master's degree

(M.A. or M.S.) or a doctorate (Ph.D.) in psychology. Social workers have earned a degree in social work. A social worker might be a L.C.S.W. (a licensed clinical social worker) or an M.S.W. (master of social work) or have a Ph.D. in social work. As with psychiatrists, insurance often covers a part of the treatment. A person who has completed training in any of these fields has had a significant amount of clinical experience under supervision. A psychoanalyst is a psychiatrist, psychologist, or social worker who has taken additional training in psychoanalysis. Psychoanalytic training can take up to ten additional years for the therapist, which ensures a greater baseline level of clinical experience. It does not ensure experience with eating disorders, however, nor does it ensure competence in other forms of treatment, like cognitive-behavioral therapy.

It is important to know that anyone can call herself a therapist or an analyst and set up a practice. She may not, however, be licensed. Unlicensed therapists may be quite empathic and kindly, and you might be tempted to see one for treatment. Don't do it. The licensing process ensures a baseline level of experience, and you should try to get the very best help you can.

How do I find someone with experience with eating disorders? Or is experience necessary?

Experience with eating disorders is important. To find someone, talk to your physician or a knowledgeable friend. You might want to get referrals from local hospitals, medical schools, graduate schools, or mental health associations. You can also contact one of the eating disorder organizations listed in Appendix 2. The National Eating Disorders Organization alone has an International Treatment Referral Directory with over nine hundred resources.

Should I interview several therapists or try to work with the first one I see?

That's a personal decision. Some people suggest interviewing several therapists prior to making a decision. If you feel comfortable with the first therapist you see, however, and that person seems to have the necessary training and experience, it's probably a good idea to go ahead and try to work with that person.

How long does therapy take?

Eating disorders often take a lifetime to develop. Complete resolution of eating disorders might take months or it might take several years.

But I don't want to spend years talking about my childhood. It wasn't much fun the first time around.

Efforts to change can only be made in the here and now, and all therapy must focus on this fact. Even in long-term psychoanalysis, current theories heavily emphasize what is going on right now, what moods and thoughts are driving you. Contrary to popular belief, therapists are often unable to find out why something happens. But patterns are often profitable to explore and can help you see what role your eating disorder currently plays in your life. And as you become more conscious of your behavior, your eating problems often fade away. So you might spend some time talking about your childhood, but you'll probably spend more time talking about what happened yesterday.

Which is better, a male therapist or a female one?

There is no right answer to this question. Some people say that young women with eating disorders should see a woman for therapy. A female therapist, they say, will more easily understand the problems that women go through in society, especially the pressure to be thin and pretty. In addition, a young woman might hand psychological power over to a male therapist and therefore not learn to take control of her life. Or she may develop a "crush" on him, which could be embarrassing and difficult.

At the same time, a female therapist can also be problematic. For example, most young women with eating disorders have conflicts with their mothers. Talking to a therapist may remind the patient of her mother, which could lead to a re-creation of old struggles.

Any of these possible problems can also be seen as an opportunity for growth. So, while you might encounter difficulties with anyone, you should probably not choose your therapist based solely on his or her gender.

But I was sexually abused as a child and am worried that a male therapist might try to abuse me. Shouldn't I go to a woman therapist?

First off, you should know that you are not alone, that many people go to see therapists after they have been sexually abused. You should also know that it is considered malpractice for a therapist to have any sort of sexual relationship with his or her patients. In some states it is even illegal, and the therapist could go to jail. You should pick a therapist with whom you are comfortable; if you are really uncomfortable talking to men, it's fine to see a female therapist. On the other hand, you might find it useful to work through your issues with a man. It's up to you.

I'm bulimic and getting ready to see a therapist. What kinds of things will we talk about?

That depends on lots of factors, including whether you see a cognitive-behavioral therapist or a therapist whose bent is more psychoanalytic or psychodynamic.

If you see a cognitive-behavioral therapist, she will

focus on your cognition (thinking) and behavior. The underlying theory is that society's emphasis on thinness has led to excess dieting, which has led to a feeling of starvation, which leads to bingeing, which leads to purging. The first aim of behavioral therapy will probably be to help you return to a normal diet. This should lead to decreased binge eating, which should lead to a decreased need to purge.

A cognitive-behavioral therapist might challenge some of your rigid rules about food and will address your distorted sense of your own body shape. She will probably discuss the factors in your environment that lead to binge eating and suggest ways to make changes. For example, you and the therapist might decide that you shouldn't be alone with binge food.

In cognitive-behavioral therapy, it is usually very important to look at your eating habits. In particular, it is important to figure out what triggers bingeing, so your individual behavior patterns will be carefully assessed. You will probably be asked to monitor your own behaviors. This type of treatment is most commonly administered by individual therapists, although group therapy can also be effective.

I've tried cognitive-behavioral therapy for my bulimia, and it seemed too impersonal, as if the therapist didn't care about me as a person. I want to work on my problems, not fill out food diaries.

Cognitive-behavioral approaches are effective for many, many people. Because they are relatively efficient, you should at least consider such a therapy. Nevertheless, cognitive-behavioral techniques by themselves leave up to half of all bulimics unsatisfied.

Psychodynamic or psychoanalytic psychotherapy is often a necessary part of the treatment. This type of treatment can include any issue in your life and can be a wonderful opportunity to explore some hidden or confusing or unhappy parts of yourself. Depending on the severity of your eating disorder, food may not be the primary focus of your sessions. Instead, you might end up talking a lot about school, family, sexuality, control, and your body. It is important to remember that most people with bulimia are not only unhappy with their eating habits, they're unhappy with themselves and their relationships. They often have high levels of anxiety and depression and low self-esteem. It can be vital to get psychotherapy that deals with the relationships between your bulimia, your feelings about yourself, and your dealings with other people. Experienced therapists can often combine cognitive-behavioral and psychodynamic therapies in a way that best suits you.

I'm anorexic. Going to a therapist feels risky to me. Why should I do something that's going to make me uncomfortable?

Psychotherapy can be instrumental in your recovery, and it can help you live a better life, but you will probably need to take a deep breath and try to trust somebody in a way that you haven't previously tried. You are probably a very private person and have undoubtedly worked very hard to present a perfect face to the world. Psychotherapy is an opportunity for you to experiment with different ways of relating, and that's a scary thing to do. It may be quite a leap of faith for you to trust a stranger and develop a partnership in which you discuss your feelings and experiences. At the same time, therapy can help you become more happy and flexible. It's up to you.

I tried therapy, and it was okay for a while, but then it just fell apart. Why should I try again?

You should try to figure out why the therapy didn't work. Maybe your first therapist focused mostly on your childhood when you needed a more cognitive-behavioral approach. Maybe your first therapist focused on tasks and goals and homework (using a cognitive-behavioral model), and you needed a more psychological approach. Maybe you just didn't have a good fit with your first (or second) therapist. Therapy can be hard work, and you need to be highly motivated to change. Maybe you weren't particularly committed to change in the past. There are many reasons therapy might have fallen apart, but that doesn't mean it will never work for you.

If you are currently in therapy and feeling misunderstood or frustrated, this can be a great opportunity for you to work on your communication skills and try to express your feelings. People with eating disorders have a strong tendency to feel misunderstood and criticized. An important part of your therapy is learning to try new ways of relating. Tell your therapist the ways in which you're unhappy with her. You might be surprised at what happens.

I'm going to see a therapist someday, but my life feels out of control. Shouldn't I wait to go into therapy until I've gotten myself better organized?

You should go to a therapist when you feel like changing your behavior, no matter how messy you may feel your life is. Therapists assume that things in your life are rocky or you wouldn't be calling in the first place.

Control may be the most important issue in your treatment. It is important to recognize that anorexia and bulimia are behaviors that have become obsessive, habitual, and self-destructive and may feel completely out of your control. Nevertheless, they are your behaviors. Therapy can help you learn to own these behaviors and take control of them.

I've been in therapy for a while, and now I binge and purge only occasionally. But my life is no better than it was before. Aren't things supposed to improve?

Bringing your eating disorder under control will not automatically make everything right in your world. Life is full of troubles. But are you sure that things are no better? Most people who binge and purge feel terribly ashamed and out of control during their cycles. You're doing better. Give yourself some credit. One thing that doesn't change immediately is the black-and-white thinking that is common in people with eating disorders. In black-and-white thinking, things are either all "good" or all "bad." Since your life isn't perfect, you may feel that stopping the bulimia hasn't made any difference. It's important to recognize that just because things aren't all good, doesn't mean they're all bad.

My bulimia was under control for two years, but lately I've been really stressed and I've started the whole binge-and-purge cycle again. Is this ever going to go away?

Relapses are common. One common reaction to a slip is to make the slip into a catastrophe. Relax. Give yourself a break. You can change your behavior, starting right now.

I'm anorexic. Somebody told me that I should see a therapist right away, and somebody else told me that therapy can be a waste of time until I've gained some weight. Who's right?

They both are, sometimes. It's hard to get any benefit from talk therapy if you are seriously malnourished. It may, however, be hard to gain any weight until psychotherapy is under way. For example, until your diet and your body distortions are addressed, you probably won't gain any weight. But simple educational techniques are generally ineffective if used by themselves. You'll need to develop some trust in someone (i.e., your therapist) before you'll be willing to accept her suggestions.

My girlfriend saw a therapist for anorexia, and it didn't work. She says the doctor totally obsessed about her weight. She got sick of hearing about it, and they ended up not even talking to each other. What happened?

Psychotherapeutic treatment of people with anorexia can be difficult. The anorexic's noneating is her best compromise for some internal problem, and the noneating becomes a very important part of her life. If a therapist insists that she immediately change her behavior, the anorexic may just shut down. In fact, she might stop talking in much the same way that she's stopped eating. Since anorexics are often in a struggle for control, it is a challenge for the therapist not to get locked in an immediate duel for supremacy. It's a duel that the anorexic almost always wins.

I went to see a therapist, and she's talking about putting me in the hospital. Why would she do that?

Hospitalization is generally recommended for anorexics who are dangerously thin. This might mean someone who weighs less than 70 percent of her normal weight or whose weight loss is out of control or who has severe lab abnormalities. In addition, people with eating disorders are sometimes hospitalized if they are suicidal, severely depressed, or dangerously self-destructive.

Is there a way to change the environment and gain structure without going to the hospital?

Yes. Many people with severe eating disorders benefit greatly from the round-the-clock treatment and supervision offered at a residential facility. There, away from family, friends, school, home life, and work, the pressures are relieved and the individual can concentrate on identifying and solving her problems.

What are hospitals and residential facilities like?

There is quite a range of offerings around the country. Generally speaking, inpatient facilities provide a controlled, structured environment in which the patient will not be allowed to "practice" her eating disorder. Nutritious, regular meals are provided; she is watched to ensure that she doesn't starve, binge, or purge; and she follows a daily schedule that helps introduce structure into her chaotic life. She'll spend much of her day learning about her eating disorder, meeting with her therapist, participating in group therapy, learning how to make positive use of her free time (time that she used to spend on eating-disordered behavior), and receiving peer support from other patients with similar issues.

If you or a loved one should enter such a facility, be aware that there will be some rules that might seem odd at first. Bathrooms are often locked after meals, for example, to reduce the frequency of vomiting. Staff may be strict, and the whole experience may be stressful for a person who is used to having her own way. Nevertheless, hospitalization and residential placement are usually quite effective at changing behaviors.

It should be noted that many insurance companies have greatly decreased their coverage of inpatient treatments for eating disorders. This has led many hospitals to eliminate their long-term inpatient treatments of people with anorexia and bulimia. The inpatient treatment programs have often been replaced by outpatient programs of various types, though some hospitals have simply eliminated their eating disorder treatment programs altogether. If you should need an inpatient program, you will probably need to work closely with your insurance company or be prepared to pay a hefty medical bill.

You mentioned that a psychiatrist might want to prescribe medications. What kind of medications might work?

Antidepressants are probably the most commonly prescribed medication for people with eating disorders. They can be helpful, for example, in slowing the binge-and-purge cycle. They are also useful in other conditions that often coexist with eating disorders, such as depression, obsessive-compulsive disorder, and panic disorder. Antidepressants include such drugs as Prozac, Zoloft, Paxil, Serzone, Effexor, Wellbutrin, Parnate, and Nardil.

How do antidepressants work? Do they cause side effects?

All the antidepressants stabilize the brain metabolism of serotonin and/or norepinephrine, which are chemicals that send messages across nerve cells. You should be aware that it takes several weeks for all the antidepressants to work, and it may be necessary to try several different antidepressants before you find one that works. All medications—including antidepressants—have possible side effects, and you should ask your doctor about side effects before taking any medication. One of the nice things about the commonly used antidepressants is that they are generally safe and well tolerated.

What other drugs might be used?

Antianxiety drugs are often useful. They have names like Valium, Ativan, and Klonopin. They are sometimes used to reduce the tension that can lead to a binge. They are generally quite safe, but they can be addictive. Unlike the antidepressants, they work right away.

Mood stabilizers have not yet been shown to help uncomplicated anorexia or bulimia. They can, however, be very useful for coexisting problems such as manic depression. The three major mood stabilizers are lithium, Tegretol (carbamazepine), and Depakote/valproic acid derivatives. Each of the mood stabilizers can be used safely by the vast majority of people, but they do require relatively careful monitoring. If you start a mood stabilizer, you will need to get regular lab work to check blood levels of the drug and to check the functioning of your kidneys, liver, and bone marrow.

Many others drugs have been tried for anorexia and bulimia. At the moment, none has been shown to be especially effective for large groups of people. Lots of research is going on, however, and your doctor may have some ideas that could work for you.

So maybe I can get better just by taking a pill?

Some bulimics have improved on medication alone. For the majority of people with bulimia, however, medication works best when combined with some form of talk therapy. So far, no medication has been very useful in treating uncomplicated cases of anorexia nervosa. Prozac has been shown in one study to help prevent relapses in people whose anorexia has already improved.

If antidepressants work by themselves sometimes, why shouldn't I just go to my internist and get a prescription?

It may be tempting to try to see your eating disorder as simply a physical problem and get some medication from your internist or gynecologist. In fact, your general medical doctor may go along with your request. Nevertheless, you should be evaluated and treated by someone who has had a lot of experience with your disorder and a lot of experience with psychiatric medication. Not only will this improve the likelihood that you'll get better, but a psychiatrist can help minimize the complications of medication side effects.

Why is group therapy important?

Group therapy, a supplement to individual therapy, offers its own unique benefits. Sometimes it's easier to understand or accept a message if it's communicated by a peer—someone who's "been there"—than if it comes from an authority figure. Led by a professional (psychologist or psychiatrist) trained to guide the discussion, group therapy can teach communication skills and assertiveness techniques, point out self-defeating behaviors, and suggest strategies for making positive changes.

Usually groups are made up of those who have the same general problems. An overweight bulimic and an anorexic, for example, may have few constructive things to say to each other.

Is group therapy the same as a support group?

No. Group therapy is led by a therapist, while support groups are run by members of the group. In addition, group therapy members pay a fee and are usually committed to the group for a certain period of time. Group therapy tends to address psychological issues with greater depth and intimacy than is found in a support group. There are some people with eating disorders (usually those with mild cases) who actually recover just by receiving the support and education they find in one of these groups.

A support group is usually set up on a "drop in" basis and does not provide therapy. Support groups inform, educate, inspire, encourage, and reach out to their members. A leader helps to structure the meetings and keep things from getting out of hand. There may be a special topic to discuss each time, or members may bring up subjects spontaneously.

There are support groups for the eating disordered as well as for their families and friends. See Appendix 2 for a list of organizations that can recommend a support group near you or can help you start one of your own.

Why should I make my family go through therapy with me?

Family therapy can teach your loved ones about eating disorders and what you're going through. It can offer them support and help them deal with their anxiety, fear, and anger. It can teach them what they're supposed to do with you, and what you're supposed to do with them. The family system often plays an important role in the eating disorder. Your family members could perhaps get better at discussing and resolving conflict. They might need to learn to communicate more directly or more empathically, or they might need to learn how to express affection. They might need to learn that the "perfect family" is a myth, or that separation doesn't necessarily mean abandonment. They might need to learn how to get more involved in your life, or they might need to learn how to back off a little. They might need to learn how to deal with you as you get better. There are many possible goals for family therapy.

I'm going to go to a family session with my daughter, but there is a secret that I'd like to keep buried. Does the therapist really need to know?

It depends a lot on what the issue is, but if it affects your daughter, you should tell the therapist. There are lots of typical family secrets. Alcohol and drug abuse, sexual abuse, and physical abuse are obvious things that people don't want to talk about. These are issues that almost always have a serious impact and need to be resolved before the child can move forward.

In addition, there are more subtle issues that a therapist will probably be interested in, and these are issues that are likely to make parents uncomfortable. Are you locked in an unhappy marriage? Do you favor one child over another? Has the family let money become too important? Do you insist that your child can't possibly be sick, that you need her to be your best friend and ally? These are issues ripe for discussion.

I've been in treatment for an eating disorder for a while, but as I've been getting better, my relationship with my husband has been falling apart. It doesn't seem fair. Any suggestions?

As people with eating disorders get better, their loved ones have to learn to adapt to the change, even if it's a change for the better. If you are anorexic, your husband may be upset that as your anorexia has improved, you have become a less perfect, dutiful wife. Or he might prefer you to be really skinny and is upset that you're at a more normal weight. If you were bulimic, as your bulimia has become resolved, your husband might unconsciously miss his impulsive, messed-up wife, a wife who always needed him to help her out. Or he might notice that you are more outgoing, happy, and attractive, and he could be jealous of the attention you're getting from other men. Or you might have become more forceful and powerful within the relationship.

This may be the time for you to seek marriage counseling. It can give both of you an opportunity to air your differences and begin working on ways to make your relationship more flexible and mature.

I've been doing the talk therapy thing until I'm blue in the face. Are there any other therapies, maybe something a little more artistic?

Yes. While the cornerstone of most treatments is talk therapy, many people are helped by therapies that focus on the creative arts. Art, dance, meditation, music, poetry, and prose can all be used to limber up a personality that has gotten locked into dysfunctional ways of being.

Chapter Six

COPING STRATEGIES
FOR FAMILIES
AND FRIENDS

And let us not be weary in well-doing;
for in due season we shall reap, if we faint not.

—Galatians 6:9

This chapter is written especially for the family and friends of an eating-disordered individual because, as you certainly know by now, she isn't traveling this road alone. You, her loved ones, want more than anything to be able to help her—yet you're not sure just what to do. You're going through excruciating pain as you watch her illness take frightening physical and psychological tolls. By turns you may feel angry, guilty, baffled, frustrated, and desperate, but most of all you're terrified at what's happening to her.

What are some of the possible reverberations within the family of an eating-disordered person?

Eating disorders can have a particularly devastating effect on families. Meals are disrupted, socializing and dining out curtailed, finances sapped, and vacation plans dictated by what the ill person will or won't do. Communication between family members suffers: parents may spend so much time focusing on their ill child that they end up ignoring their other children. Couples may neglect their marriages and each other as they concentrate solely on solving their child's eating problems. Brothers and sisters can resent the amount of time and attention that is spent on their eating-disordered sibling. As Harry Gold, father of actress Tracey Gold, put it: "This [Tracey's anorexia] has been all we've been talking about and thinking about since it came into our lives."[1]

If you're like most friends and family members of an eating-disordered person, you've tried just about everything to get through to her. Karen Carpenter's brother, Richard, certainly did, later remarking:

> I tried every approach, the gamut that people go through if they're dealing with an eating disorder victim or an alcoholic; you try heart-to-heart, yelling and screaming . . .[2]

Karen's friends also urged her to give up her eating disorder, insisting that she eat something "right now" while they watched or pleading with her to save herself.

Unfortunately, none of these approaches worked. In fact, they were all exactly the *wrong* things to do or say to try to help someone with an eating disorder. Although it's natural that you, her loved one, will want to grab control of the situation and *make* her stop, the unfortunate truth is that you'll only get caught in a power struggle that she will ultimately win. These battles for control can actually make her illness worse, and you'll end up frazzled, frustrated, and unable to concentrate on anything else. Remember, she's better at it than you are.

What can I do to help?

As a concerned family member or friend, the most important thing you can do is reassure her of your love. You can also play an instrumental role in her recovery by getting her into therapy and reinforcing the new, healthy behaviors and attitudes she'll be learning. An even more difficult (but absolutely necessary) step will be standing aside and allowing her to take responsibility for herself and her actions. Also, since eating disorders often arise in the context of a disordered family situation, family members should take this opportunity to really look at themselves. Are you overly controlling? Do you have a problem with alcohol and/or other drugs? Do you have an eating disorder yourself? Are you heavily invested in keeping your child a child so that she'll always be at your side? These issues can and should be addressed in family therapy.

This chapter will explain what you can do to help your loved one heal, giving you simple suggestions for living and dealing with an eating-disordered person *without driving yourself crazy in the process.*

A crucial first step is getting your loved one into treatment—immediately. The longer the eating-disordered behavior continues without intervention, the more entrenched it becomes and the harder it is to treat. She'll need to be checked by a physician, have a dental exam, and get a psychological evaluation. If it's recommended that she be hospitalized, encourage her to do so. In the structured environment of a hospital she may find the "time-out" she needs to break the cycle of her destructive habits.

As discussed in Chapter 5, her treatment will probably consist of medical monitoring, some form of psychotherapy, and nutritional guidance. Family therapy for those closest to her is almost always recommended and will be of great help to you. Since you and the rest of the family will be her support system (especially if she lives with you), you'll need to find out how to reinforce the new ways of coping that she'll be learning. You may also find it very helpful to see a therapist yourself to help you deal with the emotional upheaval and guide you through the many difficult situations that lie ahead.

But before any of this can happen, you'll need to

approach your loved one about her problem. This can be tricky because she will probably feel embarrassed, ashamed, or threatened if you simply confront her about it. Chances are good that she'll deny the problem, become angry, refuse help, and become even more isolated and difficult to reach. What you say to her can affect her recovery, either negatively or positively, so plan your approach carefully before plunging in.

How should I approach my loved one about her eating disorder?

In *Surviving an Eating Disorder: Strategies for Family and Friends*, author Michele Siegel et al. suggest the following tips for approaching a friend or loved one about her eating disorder:

• *Decide who is the best person to approach her*—If you are her parent, you'll probably know instinctively to whom she'll respond best—you, your spouse, or the two of you together. If you're a friend, you might want to talk with her alone or in the presence of another of her close friends. It's usually best to have no more than two people approach her; otherwise she could feel that you're ganging up on her. The chosen person should be mature (don't give this job to a child!), and someone with whom she interacts regularly and has a good rapport.

• *Pick a time when you know you won't be interrupted and you're feeling calm*—Don't try to talk to her in the middle of making dinner, while watching TV, or when someone is likely to walk in on you. Pick a quiet, relaxed time, lock the door behind you, and broach the subject in a calm, caring, supportive manner.

• *Speak with concern and compassion*—A caring and supportive approach is absolutely vital. Be clear but nonjudgmental when you tell her the behavior you've observed. For example, you might say, "I've heard you vomiting in the bathroom after meals, and I'm very concerned about you." Be as descriptive as possible when talking about her behaviors, but leave out the accusations, anger, hurt, or any other feelings that you may have. "I've noticed that you're eating less and less all the time and that you sometimes skip meals. I can see that you've lost quite a bit of weight. I'm worried about your health and also about how you're feeling emotionally." Realize that what you say will probably be embarrassing and threatening to her. If you come on too aggressively, you'll get nowhere; she'll just get defensive and try to end the discussion.

• *Don't try to talk with her when you're angry or hurt*—Whatever you do, don't bring up her eating disorder when you're in the middle of an argument with her. Already on the defensive, she'll be unlikely to listen to anything you say. It's also not a good idea to try to talk to her when you're feeling wounded, because she may end up feeling too guilty about hurting you to confide in you freely. Pick a time when you're feeling calm—you don't want the discussion to get derailed by emotion.

• *Open up the lines of communication*—Let her know that you would like to help her and that you're always ready to listen. Become an empathic listener, really trying to see things from her point of view. Take the time to sit down and focus on her when she's ready to talk, and let her take the lead. Don't negate what she says; don't get on your soapbox or try to force your views. You want her to feel free to say whatever is on her mind and to trust you with her confidences.

• *Offer to help her get into treatment*—Encourage her to get into treatment right away, before the disorder gets any worse. While it is preferable for the patient to take charge of her own therapy, you might find it necessary to make the initial appointment for her. (This is somewhat debatable, of course, since the person with the eating disorder might just see this as another example of your overinvolvement in her life.) In advance, gather all the information on eating disorders that you can find. Contact the eating disorder organizations listed in Appendix 2 and ask them to send information. Go the library or the bookstore and pick up some of the many excellent books on eating disorders. (See Recommended Reading, also in Appendix 2.) Then find out who in your area is experienced in treating eating disorders by contacting your local hospital, mental health association, or school system for referrals. Have all this information at hand when you approach her.

If she refuses, tell her that you'd like her to look at the information anyway, and that you'll be available to talk whenever she's ready. Unless she is dangerously ill, it is best to let her think about it for a while. Remember that treatment is much more successful when *she* decides that she needs it. Another option is for family members to get into therapy, even if the eating-disordered person does not. You may wish to see a therapist by yourself, husband and wife might see a couples therapist, and/or the entire family could get involved in family therapy. Once the eating-disordered family member sees that the rest of you are willing to look at your own behavior, she may be more likely to take a look at her own.

• *Negotiate a plan of acceptable behavior*—This applies primarily to parents who have an eating-disordered daughter living in their home. If she refuses to get treatment or thinks she can handle the problem on her own, work with her to draw up a "contract" that specifies what kinds of foods she should eat and how many meals a day are acceptable. Bingeing or purging must decrease or completely stop, and exercise should be done moderately. The contract should also spell out a specific period of time that she'll be given to implement these new behaviors. After that, if she can't live up to the terms of the contract, she must agree to get professional help.

• *Get immediate help for her if she is in trouble*—Whether you are a parent, a teacher, or a friend, get professional help for her immediately (no matter what she says) if she is:

1. Binge eating, purging, or starving to the point where she's too weak or sick to function effectively
2. Unable to keep any food in her stomach
3. Engaging in self-mutilation, substance abuse, promiscuity, tantrums, etc.
4. Suicidal[3]

Eating disorders can be deadly. Most victims can't see themselves or their situations clearly enough to know what to do. They are depending on *you* to recognize the danger signs and pull them back from the brink.

If you think your friend has an eating disorder, should you tell her parents?

Approach your friend in the supportive manner described above, tell her of your concern, and suggest that she see her doctor, the school nurse, or a counselor, or contact an eating disorder organization to get help. Gather as much information as you can, and give it to her. Offer to make appointments for her and even accompany her to these appointments if she wants. If she continues to do nothing, tell her parents. They should be advised of their daughter's life-threatening behavior. Often parents are completely unaware of their child's eating disorder until it's well entrenched, especially if she's no longer living with them. Once you have informed her parents, if they do nothing about the situation, contact your school nurse, a counselor, or any of the treatment organizations listed in Appendix 2 to ask for help.

Should a True Friend Tell?

Carolyn Bartholomew was one of the late Princess Diana's closest friends, dating back to when they were children at boarding school. Carolyn knew about Diana's bulimia, observing her friend with growing concern as her illness grew worse. Finally, when Carolyn read that the loss of certain minerals through vomiting could be the cause of the tiredness and depression that plagued her friend, she called Diana and urged her to see a doctor. Diana balked, saying that she "didn't have the will to discuss her problems with a specialist." But Carolyn issued an ultimatum: Either Diana would see a doctor about her eating disorder, or Carolyn would tell the press that Diana was bulimic.

Reluctantly Diana made an appointment, which became the first of many steps along the road to her recovery. After six months of treatment she told Carolyn that she felt she'd been "born again." Her old routine of inducing vomiting four times a day had already been reduced to once every three weeks.[4]

You may feel that you're betraying your friend by telling her parents about her eating disorder or taking other steps to ensure that she gets help. In truth, you may be saving her life. Like Carolyn Bartholomew, friends are often in a much better position than family members to see trouble brewing. By being the first to sound the alarm, you might well be able to help your friend stop her eating disorder in its tracks—before it causes permanent damage.

I want to be of help to my daughter, but some days I'm so upset and depressed I can barely function myself . . .

Living with someone who has an eating disorder can be very stressful, especially for parents or other loved ones. In either case, some form of therapy can be very useful. Family therapy, individual therapy, and support groups can each play an important role in the patient's recovery. While it is sometimes done, it is generally *not* recommended that you see the patient's therapist for individual therapy. The complications of such an arrangement usually outweigh the convenience. When a therapist sees two people *for individual therapy* who are involved with each other, it becomes almost impossible to get beyond issues of confidentiality and favoritism. For *family therapy*, of course, everyone sees one therapist, and the family as a group becomes the "patient." If at all possible, make use of a family therapist for everyone, but get your own individual therapist.

Support groups can offer a great deal of assistance to those who are living and dealing with eating-disordered individuals. People who face problems and situations similar to yours can be an invaluable source of understanding, coping strategies, and advice. If you can't find such a support group in your area, it may be well worth your while to start one yourself. The National Eating Disorders Organization (NEDO) is a terrific source of information on how to start your own support group. (See Appendix 2.)

Besides finding a source of support for yourself, try hard to maintain as much normalcy in your life as possible. It's a common mistake to get so caught up in your loved one's problems that your own health, hobbies, work, relationships, and leisure activities are pushed aside. Make sure that you eat properly, exercise regularly, get plenty of sleep, and use stress-releasing techniques daily. Continue working, spending time on hobbies, seeing friends, and having fun. Staying home and obsessing about your loved one's problems doesn't help and may well make things worse for the entire family.

Other family members should also attend to their own needs and carry on normal activities. Try not to give the eating-disordered individual special privileges or let family life revolve around her problems. She should be held responsible for her own behavior, and all siblings should be treated fairly and equally. Treating her like a pampered baby will work against her recovery, prolonging the life of her disorder.

What emotional changes might I go through as her eating disorder progresses?

The loved ones of an eating-disordered person often go through a series of stages as they witness the progress of the disease. These are remarkably similar to Elisabeth Kübler-Ross's five stages of dying—emotional changes that a person experiences as she learns to accept her situation. They are *denial*, *anger*, *bargaining*, *depression*, and *acceptance*.

• *Denial*—During this stage, the loved ones of the eating-disordered individual first become aware of the problem. They may try to dismiss it, minimize its importance, or flat out deny its existence. They'll say, "She's just being hysterical" (or silly, stubborn, etc.) or "She'll stop all this nonsense as soon as she gets a little older" (or goes to college, gets married, wises up, etc.) or "By next week she'll be on to something else."

• *Anger*—As the problem becomes more visible and it's apparent that she isn't going to stop, they'll become frightened, asking, "Why is she doing this?" "Why can't she quit?" Then the fright is masked by anger: "If she loved me, she'd stop hurting me this way." "She's ruining her life and ours!" "She's throwing away her health for no good reason!"

- *Bargaining*—Rewards may be offered to entice her to give up her disordered behavior. "If you'll gain weight, I'll buy you a whole new wardrobe." "If you'll stop purging for two months, I'll take you to Europe." Parents may issue ultimatums: "If you don't stop doing this, I'm not paying for college." They may even try to strike bargains with God: "Lord, if You'll take away this disease, I'll never ask for anything else again."

- *Depression*—When nothing seems to stem the tide of her illness, loved ones may fall into deep depression. They'll ask themselves, "Why isn't she well yet?" They'll say, "I feel so helpless. Nothing I do seems to make her get better"; "I can't stand to watch her getting worse"; "I've lost interest in everything. Nothing can make me happy when she's so sick."

- *Acceptance*—Finally they realize that they can't change her; they can only love and support her. They must reconcile themselves to the fact that her eating behaviors and her recovery belong to her alone. "I accept that I am doing the best I can to help her, but she is responsible for her own recovery."

In Cherry Boone O'Neill's book *Starving for Attention*, her husband, Dan, wrote movingly about his own journey through the five stages, adding one more of his own—hope:[5]

- *Denial*—Dan and Cherry began their married life filled with high hopes and lofty dreams. Although Cherry had been plagued with anorexia for several years, they believed that it was now a thing of the past. They gave testimonials of healing at banquets, at church services, and on TV talk shows. Unfortunately it soon became obvious that Cherry had not recovered; she had just become more adept at hiding the signs of her eating disorder. As her health began to deteriorate, both Dan and Cherry tried to deny the obvious. "We were afraid to even consider relapse as a possibility. . . . We just denied the facts and closed our eyes, hoping that this thing would just go away. . . ."

• *Anger*—When Dan finally had to admit to himself that Cherry was again practicing her eating disorder (although she denied it vehemently), he became furious. "A kind of anger I had never known began to well up inside. . . . How could she lie to me, her own husband? . . . 'Are you an animal or a human being?' I demanded. 'You've got a brain—use it!' "

• *Bargaining*—Dan began to think that maybe a reward system would work. He told Cherry (who was 97 pounds at the time), "If you will just get your weight up to 105 pounds, I'll take you to Jerusalem and Rome on my upcoming business trip." The result? No weight gain. In fact, even more precious pounds were lost. Not only did the bargaining technique fail, it proved to be counterproductive.

• *Depression*—When Cherry had to be hospitalized, Dan plunged into a deep depression, believing that hers was a terminal case. "I had dreams of swimming in an unlighted tank full of black ink," he writes. "I was drowning—helpless to alter what seemed to be certain tragedy."

• *Acceptance*—Believing that he was powerless to change the situation, Dan felt he had no other choice than to give up. He was surprised to learn from Cherry's doctor that this could actually be a positive step. "Though I still loved Cherry, I had to release her to choose her own destiny—even if that choice meant death."

• *Hope*—Finally, after much therapy, Cherry and her doctor were able to turn a corner in her illness. "The key word is *process*," Dan wrote. Without hope, Dan is certain they wouldn't have made it. But today Cherry is completely recovered, and she and Dan are the proud parents of five children.

While you're still in denial, furious, depressed, or striking bargains, you, like Dan O'Neill, probably won't be of much help to your loved one. Instead you'll find yourself tangled up in power struggles, guilt trips, and other fruitless endeavors. Friends and relatives of an eating-disordered person understandably feel panicked at what's happening to their loved one. They may go through a long period of trying to "fix" her. Unfortunately they can't, and in the process they can make the problem even worse.

But I can't stand by and just let her starve herself . . .

Once your loved one is in treatment, the most important thing that you can do to help her recover is to *let go*. Undoubtedly, this is the last thing you want to do right now. Your natural instinct is to grab control of the situation and get your loved one back on course. But it's absolutely crucial to her recovery that you learn to *disengage from her problem*. The more you try to exert control, the more you try to "fix" her, the more you try to make everything right, the longer it will take for her to get well. One of the reasons that she developed an eating disorder in the first place was that she needed to feel that she was in control of some part of her life. If you try to snatch back control, it will only make everything worse.

Disengaging from your loved one's eating disorder means giving up the idea that you can somehow control her behavior, and thereby solve her problems. It means allowing her to be in charge of her own eating. And it means letting the responsibility for her behavior and her recovery lie where it belongs—with the eating-disordered individual herself.

How do you "disengage" from the eating disorder?

Once she is in treatment, get out of the way and let her heal. Stop begging, threatening, yelling, or encouraging her to eat. Stop focusing on food and start encouraging your loved one to take responsibility for her own actions. She's not a young child anymore; she must learn to face the consequences of her behavior. *Until you and she can do this, it's unlikely that she will make much progress.*

To Disengage from the Eating Disorder:

• *Accept that you can't "fix" her—it's beyond your ability.*

Eating disorders are complex psychological problems, difficult even for professionals to treat. Your loved one has been using eating behaviors as a way to cope with her problems. She won't change until she acquires a whole new set of constructive coping behaviors and ways of thinking. The ability to soothe herself, express her feelings, or feel good about herself may be missing in her psychological makeup—all these issues will be addressed in her therapy sessions. You cannot and should not try to tackle these problems yourself. Your job is to provide her with love and support, not to try to "make" her well.

• *Allow her to be in charge of her eating.*

The bottom line is that *she* is the one who ultimately decides what goes into her mouth. You can threaten, cry, lay on the guilt trips, or offer bribes, but in the end she'll control her own eating. The sooner you realize that battles over food are no-win situations, the better for everyone.

Food has taken on a symbolic meaning in her life, and she'll have to learn to separate it from all her other issues. The more you interfere with her food behaviors, the harder it will be for her to distinguish between food behaviors and her emotions. If you are her parent, your food responsibilities should be limited to providing nourishing, tasty meals. Period. She is responsible for feeding herself. If you are a friend, you have no food responsibilities.

- *Realize that recovery is her responsibility—*
not yours.

No one can force her to recover. Recovery is a difficult, often painful process that requires full commitment and plenty of hard work. The will to recover must come from the inside, not the outside. You can only encourage her, persuade her that a healthy, normal life is worth working for, and set a good example by taking care of your own health. She must do the rest.

Disengaging certainly doesn't mean that you no longer care about what she does or what happens to her. It's vital that you *do* care and that you remain a constant source of love and support. Disengaging simply means that you decline to get involved in battles over her eating behavior.

What can I do to disengage from the eating disorder while continuing to be there for her?

Do

1. *Listen to her as nonjudgmentally and calmly as you can*—Try not to get defensive when she blames *you* for her problems. Accept that her point of view is simply the way she remembers things—even if you remember them differently. She needs to work through these issues so she can learn to forgive those who have hurt her. Eventually she should get to the point where she can listen to you in a nonjudgmental way, too.

2. *Accept her right to choose her own food*—This means not only refraining from making comments about her food or eating, but being careful of your body language too. Sighing, grimacing, tightening your lips, rolling your eyes, or raising your eyebrows can communicate

just as much as a disparaging comment. Hard as it is, you've got to let her take charge of her eating.

3. *Learn all you can about eating disorders*—Educate yourself, read the literature, attend support groups, ask your therapist questions. The more you know, the better equipped you will be to help your loved ones and yourself.

4. *Let her know you care about her as a person*—Make sure she knows that you love her and that your love is *not* determined by her weight, shape, or looks. Be careful not to comment on her appearance in either negative *or* positive ways. ("Wow, you look great!" may be taken as "You're getting fat.") Take the focus off looks, and focus on the positive aspects of her character as much as possible.

5. *Respect her privacy*—It will be tempting for you to try to assess how much she's eating, to check her bedroom for food "stashes," to look for evidence of bingeing or purging, or to read her journal to figure out what's going on in her mind. Don't.

6. *Give her time to recover*—It takes two to five years of treatment for the average eating disorder patient to recover. Don't expect instant progress. Be patient.

7. *Leave the guilt behind*—Neither you nor anyone else is to blame for the eating disorder—it's the result of a complex combination of factors. Guilt is not only inappropriate in this case, it's paralyzing. Put your energy into positive actions instead.

8. *Be gentle with yourself*—Give yourself credit for doing the best you can. Don't expect that you will always do or say the right thing. You're human, and no one (including you) should expect you to be perfect.

Don't

1. *Monitor her eating behavior once she's in treatment.* Don't try to figure out how much she's eating, hover over her as she eats, stop her from eating too much, or otherwise "breathe down her neck" about food and eating behaviors. Refrain from making remarks, even encouraging ones, about what she is or isn't eating. The best thing you can do is ignore her eating (or the lack of it). One of her major tasks in therapy will be learning how to monitor her own behavior. Let her try, and fail if need be, until she learns—no matter how many times it takes.

2. *Bargain with her or use scare tactics*—Telling her "I'll buy you a new outfit if you don't binge for a week" or "The next time I hear you throwing up, I'll ground you" misses the point by encouraging her to focus only on the outcome rather than the process. Any decrease in symptoms will be only temporary, for the control comes from external sources rather than internal. Bargaining and/or scare tactics will usually make the illness much worse by inflaming her resentment and desire for control.

3. *Shame her into changing her behavior*—She already feels terrible about herself and guilty about the pain she's inflicting on those around her. Shaming her will only lower her self-esteem further and cause her to withdraw.

4. *Pity her*—Your pity will also undermine her self-esteem, making her feel that she's incapable of acting like a normal person. Instead, try to provide opportunities for her to take responsibility and develop independence.

5. *Suggest what she should or shouldn't eat*—Avoid giving advice, opinions, or guidance when it comes to eating. Don't try to control her food choices, the amounts she eats, or even whether or not she eats. Avoid making special meals for her, tempting her with favorite foods,

portioning out her food, or otherwise attempting to control her intake. What she eats is *her* business.

6. *Use money to try to control eating behavior*—Do not offer her money for pounds lost, food eaten, or behavior changed. This is another external method of controlling an internal problem. It won't work for long, if at all, and is sure to backfire eventually.

7. *Tell her she looks too thin*—She will probably take this as a compliment and redouble her dieting efforts. In fact, stay away from all discussions about looks; focus on her other qualities instead.

8. *Praise her for gaining weight*—She may panic and think she's getting fat. She could also feel that *you* have won and she has lost, even though weight gain may be in her best interest. Karen Carpenter once made a needlepoint picture for her therapist that said, "You win, I gain."

9. *Try to be her therapist*—When she comes to you with food and weight-related problems, tell her that you'd like to help her but that it's better for her to discuss these issues with her therapist. You should not have to be worried about saying the proper thing or eliciting the proper response from her to help her heal. She may ask your opinion of how she looks, or whether she's too fat or too thin. Sidestep these looks- or weight-related issues; they're no-win situations. Once you start giving advice and opinions, you can easily get caught up in the control game again. It is fine, of course, to have meaningful adult conversations with her. These talks can be on any topic and may involve how she's feeling or how you're feeling. The point is that you shouldn't try to be her therapist or cheerleader.

How will I know whether I've truly disengaged from her eating disorder?

Even if you're scrupulously following the suggestions listed above, overinvolvement may still be a problem. If you answer yes to any of the following questions, you may still need to work on letting go:

- Does your mood depend on how much your loved one weighs or how well she's eating that day?
- Are you secretly on the lookout for signs that she's starving, bingeing, or purging (e.g., scrupulously noting what she eats or doesn't eat, checking her purse for laxatives, listening at the bathroom door)?
- Do you find yourself constantly thinking about her eating problems or neglecting your other duties because you're so worried or distracted?

If you're having difficulty disengaging from the eating disorder, ask your therapist or support group to help you find out why. Perhaps you're focusing on the disorder to distract yourself from other problems, such as a troubled marriage, alcoholism, or physical abuse. Perhaps you need to fill a void in your life or to feel that you're needed. Ask yourself, "What would I be thinking about if the eating disorder didn't exist?"

My bulimic daughter can eat up all the food in our kitchen in one binge. Am I supposed to just ignore it when it happens?

Absolutely not. Disengaging from an eating disorder means putting responsibility where it belongs. Just as each person is responsible for feeding herself, the eating-disordered person is also responsible for any adverse effects her behavior has on others, *whether she can control it or not*. For example, if a binger eats up all of the family's food, she must take responsibility for her actions, replacing that food with her own money. If a purger messes up the family bathroom, she must clean it up immediately so that others aren't inconvenienced. An excessive exerciser should not be allowed to exercise late at night if it disturbs the sleep of others in the house.

Be very clear about the responsibilities she has to you and the other people in the house. Similarly, she may have requests for you or other family members. For example, you might want her to be responsible for stocking the kitchen, and she might want you to keep the kitchen clean. A compromise can be made and a contract drawn up. (This is perfect material for a family session.) Once the contract is drawn up, the family should follow through with it as scrupulously as possible. The failure of any party to stick to the contract will be a great opportunity to look further into the family dynamics and structure.

What household rules should we set up?

When living with an eating-disordered person, your primary goal should be to maintain as much normalcy in the family as possible. She may be behaving in crazy, destructive ways, but you and the rest of the family don't have to get sucked into them. By disengaging from the eating problem, you remove responsibility for her actions and recovery from your shoulders and put it back on hers, where it belongs. While she and her therapist do the inner work that will help her recover, your responsibilities are limited to four things:

- Be supportive.
- Avoid doing and saying things that exacerbate the disorder.
- Get into treatment yourself.
- Safeguard the health and happiness of your family.

It's easy to forget this last point. You may be so worried about her that you neglect the "healthy" family members. This is not only unfair, it increases the risk that they will develop serious problems of their own later on. The family should *not* revolve around the eating-disordered member. She should fit in with the family. With that in mind, consider the following dos and don'ts:

Do

1. *Negotiate acceptable behavior with her*—She should not be allowed to lock herself in the bathroom for hours while other family members wait. Decide on an appropriate time limit and insist that she stick to it— *not* because you are trying to prevent her from purging, but because it's unfair to other family members. She should also perform her regular chores and attend to her normal family responsibilities as well as she can.

2. *Make her responsible for her own behavior*—If she's a binger, she must replace her binge foods. If she doesn't have any money, she should do household chores until she has "worked off" her debt. If she purges and leaves the bathroom in a mess, she must clean it up. Don't end up taking on the responsibility yourself. She needs to learn, as part of her growing-up process, that her behavior has consequences.

3. *Invite her to join you for meals*—If she says she's not eating, tell her that you'd like her company anyway. If she still refuses, don't make an issue of it. Simply say, "Okay, but we'll miss you." Then when the next mealtime rolls around, invite her again. Keep inviting her so that she knows she's welcome. Sooner or later she may join you.

4. *Encourage family members to air their feelings*— Family members can bottle up their feelings of anger, resentment, and frustration, causing bigger problems later on. To counteract this, establish weekly family meetings during which all can have their say about what's going on and suggest changes. Remember that each family member is as important as any other, and the feelings of all should be respected.

5. *Show verbal and physical affection often*—Let each family member know that he or she is loved. Hugs, kisses, and words of appreciation or endearment are vital to everyone's emotional well-being.

Don't

1. *Let the eating-disordered member dictate what, when, or where the family will eat*—The family should maintain normal eating patterns, no matter what the eating-disordered member is doing. Family members should eat what they typically eat, at the times and in the places to which they're accustomed. Don't suddenly start serving "diet meals" because your eating-disordered family member is more likely to eat them, or stop serving dessert because she might binge on it.

2. *Prepare "special" meals for her*—If she wants to prepare her own meal, that's all right, but don't get caught up in trying to accommodate her dietary whims. Like other family members, she should be free to eat what you've prepared for everyone but be able to get her own food if she'd rather. Otherwise, you're setting yourself up for control battles when she refuses to eat what you've so carefully prepared.

3. *Keep certain foods out of the house because she's likely to binge on them*—You'll probably be tempted to let her eating disorder dictate which foods you will or won't buy, but don't fall into this trap. Everyone in the family should be able to have the foods they want, regardless of the temptation they might pose to the anorexic or binger. She will simply have to face her problem and find ways to deal with it, or take responsi-

bility for her actions. If you create a false environment for her (with locked cabinets, no tempting foods, etc.), she won't have to develop the inner resources that she needs to handle her problems.

At the same time, an out-of-control binger may need a little extra support in the beginning, so it is probably advisable to help her identify the foods that trigger her binges and remove them from sight. This is an example of a family compromise. While other members of the family shouldn't be enormously inconvenienced by any one person, each person should have the right to request small favors from others in the household.

4. *Argue at the table*—Mealtimes shouldn't be a battleground, even if the battles aren't about food per se. Arguing, complaining, venting, or disciplining at the table can turn eating into a negative experience for all involved. Strive to keep the conversation light and make mealtimes pleasant, positive experiences.

Is there anything else I can do to help her recover?

Yes—keep loving her and reaching out to her. Mother Teresa once said, "The most important medicine is tender love and care." By communicating your constant love and support *and not giving up*, you may do more to stem the tide of your loved one's illness than you ever imagined. As Carolyn Costin notes in *The Eating Disorder Sourcebook*, "People who have recovered from eating disorders often cite being loved, believed in, and not given up on as crucial factors in their getting help and getting well."[6]

Once your loved one is in treatment, it's essential that you continue to be as caring and supportive as possible while still acting as natural as possible. Don't bring up eating, diets, her weight, or her appearance, although it's usually fine to talk matter-of-factly about these issues (or about anything). Don't even tell her how much better she looks now (she'll assume you mean she looks fat) or how bad she's looked in the past. Focus on the person rather than her appearance. Remember that she will be feeling intensely inadequate. If she picks up any signs that you're impatient, disgusted, or scornful, her symptoms will be intensified. What she needs most now is simply your love and support.

As you continue to fight the good fight, remember to take good care of yourself and your family, seek help from a therapist or a support group, and give it time. With you squarely behind her, your loved one is surely on her way to regaining strength, health, and happiness.

Chapter Seven

PREVENTION: WHAT YOU CAN DO TO KEEP YOUR CHILD FROM DEVELOPING AN EATING DISORDER

An ounce of prevention is worth a pound of cure.
—Benjamin Franklin

Are there ways to prevent eating disorders in the first place?

A child's relationship with you and with food begins at birth. It is important to respect the fact that your infant is trying to gain comfort in the world and that she needs to develop a sense of control over her environment. Let your child dictate how much food she eats. In the early days, feed her when she seems hungry. Eventually the two of you can set up a routine. Let her decide how fast she eats. Give her time to pause when she wants. If she gets upset during feeding, soothe her and then let her try to eat again. She may still be hungry.

But won't that make her spoiled?

The most important thing to keep in mind is that your infant has a lot of work to do on the way to becoming a mature adult. Part of the work involves growing into an independent person who can also feel very intimate with others. To do this she'll need to develop a sense that she can (at least somewhat) control the world around her. Early on, the things she needs are food, shelter, and lots of love. If she feels she has some say in getting these needs met, she'll begin to develop trust in others and a strong sense of self.

Is it better to breast-feed or bottle-feed?

It depends on your situation. For most women, breast-feeding is preferable because breast milk has some important antibodies that can help protect the baby from infection. Breast-feeding can be an enormously intimate experience between mother and child. And breast milk is free. Nevertheless, many women choose not to breast-feed. This might be because they are taking medications that can get into the breast milk, for example, or there are mechanical problems (like infection), or breast-feeding just doesn't seem to be the thing the mother wants to do. While breast-feeding is recommended, bottle-feeding can be a perfectly acceptable substitute.

I'm breast-feeding. How do you control the amount of milk that gets to the baby?

As long as your baby is sucking, doesn't seem hungry afterward, and is growing adequately, you're doing fine. Milk production is controlled by your baby's needs. The more milk your baby takes from the breast, the more will be produced next time. Pay attention to what's happening, but try not to get too worried about it. Don't forget that women have been breast-feeding since the human race began and things generally work out fine. But if you're having troubles, don't hesitate to ask an expert. The "expert" could be a friend, a representative of La Leche League, or one of the breast-feeding specialists found at many hospitals.

Any suggestions for bottle-feeding?

The principles are the same. Cradle your baby and pay attention to the signs that she's had enough. Mothers are generally the experts on whether their infants are hungry or tired or have a dirty diaper, but this is not a "sixth sense" that is automatically acquired. You need to pay attention to your child and gradually develop a give-and-take that can be a great experience for both of you.

If you're bottle-feeding, follow the directions carefully. Some people try to adjust the formula, but this isn't a good idea. Don't water it down in hopes of having a thin child. This can cause malnutrition and failure to thrive, not to mention an unhappy baby. A baby who always feels hungry is also likely to overeat later when she can get to the food supply.

Lots of mothers add extras to the formula, like chocolate, syrup, sugar, flavored gelatin, and especially cereal to help their children "sleep through the night." Don't do it! These can lead to obesity, poor nutrition, and rotten teeth. In short, follow the directions. Save your creativity for your interactions with your child and the rest of the family.

When is it the right time to start solid foods?

You should start solid foods when your child is ready for them. You'll know this because she'll sit up, drool, and open her mouth when she sees food approaching. She'll no longer thrust solid food out of her mouth with her tongue; she'll use her tongue to push the food to the back of her throat where she can swallow it. Your child will probably be ready for solid foods between the ages of four and seven months. Don't force it. Feeding solids too early can cause allergies, digestive problems, and obesity.

What can be done during childhood to prevent eating disorders?

Most children will automatically take in sufficient calories for growth and maintenance just by obeying their hunger and satiety signals—that is, if you let them! Parents sometimes try to manipulate a child's body weight by over- or underfeeding. This usually backfires. Those who are forced to eat more than they want may develop an aversion to food, finding ways to undereat whenever possible. The underfed, on the other hand, can become preoccupied with food, making it more likely that they'll binge when they do find a food source.

Leslie, who was a skinny child, tells horror stories about being forced to eat everything on her plate within a certain time limit. Her mother insisted that if she didn't finish her food within twenty minutes, she would start piling more on Leslie's plate. Her mother continued to add more food to the plate every twenty minutes until it was all eaten. Not surprisingly, Leslie eventually became anorexic, insisting that she hated eating and that food "made her sick."

Rolanda's father was a successful television writer struggling to raise his daughter alone. Under intense pressure at work and at home, he tended to be impatient and overly controlling even though he loved his daughter very much. But when she began to get a little chubby at age nine, he panicked. He sternly warned her away from cookies, chips, cheese, and anything else he deemed "fattening," and started monitoring everything she ate. During the summer, he sent her off to a weight-control camp for nine weeks.

When Rolanda returned from camp, she *had* slimmed down, but the weight came back almost immediately, plus an additional ten pounds soon after. Furious at her lack of "self-control," Rolanda's father began locking the kitchen cabinets. But it seemed that the more he pushed her to lose weight, the more weight she gained.

By age eighteen, Rolanda weighed 250 pounds and had completely cut off communication with her father.

As with infants, it's vitally important to let a child's hunger and satiety signals dictate how much she eats, even if her natural body shape isn't what you'd prefer aesthetically. Once you try to manipulate her intake to make her look a certain way, you're courting disaster. Of course, that doesn't mean that you, her caretaker, should allow her to eat anything and everything at all times of the day or night. You *will* need to exert a certain amount of control over what, where, and when she eats to help her regulate her intake.

How can I help my child regulate her food intake?

According to Ellyn Satter, R.D., there is a "division of responsibility" between parents and children in the feeding relationship:

- The parent is responsible for what is presented to eat.
- The child is responsible for how much she eats or even *whether* she eats.[1]

Your job as a parent is to provide nutritious, attractive, appealing foods that your child can manage at her stage of development. The food should be evenly distributed throughout the day so that she'll be hungry when she comes to the table, but not starving. (Three meals and one or two snacks will usually do the trick.) Balanced meals containing protein, carbohydrate, and some fat will help regulate her blood sugar and keep her feeling satisfied.

Eating should be limited to a specific area where nothing else takes place (i.e., at the table rather than in front of the TV, in bed, on the couch, etc.). When meals are taken, there should be no accompanying distractions—no books, toys, television, videos, etc. She should concentrate on eating, enjoying her food, and taking pleasure in the company of whoever is eating with her.

Watch carefully for cues that she has either had enough or wants more food, and act accordingly. Once the meal is over, all food should be put away and forgotten until the next meal or snack. The idea is to enjoy eating, savor the food and the experience of eating, stop eating when satisfied, then forget about food until next time. Children who get in the habit of eating this way are more likely to eat according to internal cues rather than external cues, and less likely to develop food obsessions.

What about the child who will eat only a few kinds of foods?

Once again your role as a parent or caretaker is to provide a variety of nutritious foods; the child's job is to decide what she will eat. You should try to include some of her favorites in each meal, prepared in ways that she likes, but don't force her to eat anything. If you're careful to provide foods that are highly nutritious (avoiding candy, cakes, pies, and other junk food), then whatever she chooses will be of some value. Remember: Children eat best when parents don't push them. Assume that her tastes and preferences are normal and go along with them while continuing to offer nutritious, well-balanced meals.

Are there any other things that I can do to help my child avoid an eating disorder?

Yes! You can begin by modeling a healthy lifestyle. If *you* have healthful eating habits, exercise regularly, manage stress properly, don't abuse substances, and treat your spouse and other family members with love and respect, your children will be more likely to adopt these habits themselves.

Other things you can do to help prevent eating disorders:

- De-emphasize "looks" when you describe yourself, your child, or others.
- Get your child into the habit of exercising three or four times a week. (Set a good example by doing the same.)
- Teach your child good nutrition habits. Buy and serve healthful foods.
- Plan family outings that don't involve eating and are exercise-oriented, such as hiking, skating, and bicycling.
- Talk to older children about the media's obsession with thinness. Limit the amount of time your children spend watching television, since it encourages sedentary lifestyles, consumption of junk food, and unrealistic standards of beauty.
- Avoid using food as a reward or a punishment.
- Involve the whole family in preparing meals several nights a week. Then sit down to eat together, without the distractions of TV, books, phone calls, etc.
- Always focus on health rather than weight.
- Set goals for your child that emphasize growth rather than perfection.
- Think twice before getting your child involved on a competitive level in sports, hobbies, or careers that emphasize looks and thinness (e.g., gymnastics, ballet, figure skating, modeling, or acting).
- Don't put your child on a diet or otherwise push her to lose weight.

What can I do to keep my teenager from developing an eating disorder?

When a child becomes a teenager, she enters an impressionable period of life during which body dissatisfaction hits an all-time high. Teenage girls are particularly vulnerable to developing eating disorders because their self-esteem is closely linked to weight and looks. It's important to talk to your teenager about the pressure she may feel to have the "perfect body." Discuss the billion-dollar dieting and fashion industries that make their money by preying on women's insecurities. Point out how unrealistic and unhealthy the images in fashion magazines are—most of those women don't carry enough body fat to sustain menstruation. Talk with her about society's thinness mania and the silly idea that being thin is the key to happiness, success, and love. Discuss such possible role models as Eleanor Roosevelt or Barbara Jordan, whose contributions to society have been based on their intelligence, values, and good works rather than their looks. Remind her that people come in all shapes and sizes, and that looks are a poor indication of a person's worth.

The Basic Tenets of Health at Every Size, developed by dietitians and nutritionists, can be used as a springboard for your discussions:

Basic Tenets of Health at Every Size[2]

- Human beings come in a variety of sizes and shapes. We celebrate this diversity as a positive characteristic of the human race.

- There is no ideal body size, shape, or weight that every individual should strive to achieve.

- Every body is a good body, whatever its size or shape.

- Self-esteem and body image are strongly linked. Helping people feel good about their bodies and about who they are can help motivate them to maintain healthy behaviors.

- Appearance stereotyping is inherently unfair to the individual because it is based on superficial factors over which the individual has limited control.

- We respect the bodies of others even though they might be quite different from our own.
- Each person is responsible for taking care of his or her body.
- Good health is not defined by body size; it is a state of physical, mental, and social well-being.
- People of all sizes and shapes can reduce their risk of poor health by adopting a healthy lifestyle.

Is there anything special that a father can do to help his daughter avoid eating disorders?

Fathers can do much to prevent the onset of eating disorders in their daughters. A dad's love and support can be crucial to a girl's successful transition from girlhood to womanhood. When girls enter adolescence, their need for male approval reaches an all-time high. They often attempt to control their bodies and their weight to gain approval, affection, and acceptance from the men in their lives, including their fathers. By praising her other attributes, helping to build and maintain her self-esteem, and stressing that a person's value is based on inner qualities rather than looks, a father can help immunize his daughter against "thinness disease." More specifically, a dad can help his daughter avoid eating disorders by:[3]

- Letting her know that he loves her, no matter what she weighs.
- Helping to build her self-esteem by showing her his approval, respect, and trust.
- Really listening to her rather than simply trying to push his beliefs on her, and respecting her growing individuality.
- Loving and respecting her mother, and working hard to make their marriage a good example of what a relationship should be.
- Sharing household chores to show his daughter that

men and women are equal partners who work
together and respect each other.

- Refraining from making negative comments about
  his daughter's appearance, other women's bodies, or
  women in general. (If he puts other women down,
  his daughter will feel slighted too.)
- Downplaying the importance of appearance, and
  emphasizing inner qualities instead.
- Helping her to define her values and see what is
  really important about other people.
- Encouraging her and offering her the same
  opportunities that he would offer a boy. He should
  guard against giving her the impression that women
  are lesser beings or that they don't need to know
  certain things.
- Spending time with her. She needs to know that he's
  interested and he cares. This will mean more to her
  than he'll ever know.

Remember that women and girls who feel good
about themselves, who feel loved, respected, listened to,
and valued, don't have to diet to prove their worth.
Your daughter depends on *you*, her parents, to help her
develop the strong sense of self that will help her resist
the lure of all destructive coping behaviors.

What can coaches, trainers, or dance teachers do to help prevent eating disorders?

Athletes and dancers are especially at risk for developing eating disorders. Even if they perform well, they can
be "marked down" if they don't conform to the ideal
body size, shape, or weight for their sport or art. This
extra pressure to be thin is reflected in the prevalence of
eating disorders among athletes. While only 1 percent
of the general female population meets the diagnostic
criteria for anorexia, and another 1 to 3 percent for

bulimia, studies estimate that 15 to 62 percent of female athletes exhibit disordered eating behaviors and attitudes.[4] Most at risk are gymnasts, cheerleaders, divers, figure skaters, swimmers, tennis players, runners, wrestlers, dancers, and those involved in equestrian sports.

Adding more fuel to the fire, many coaches and trainers believe that reducing body fat really can enhance performance. Even though studies have shown that this isn't necessarily true, an athlete or a dancer who doesn't perform well is often automatically told to lose weight, and quickly. This pressure can bring on desperate, destructive weight-control behaviors, especially if the athlete or dancer is trying to reach or maintain a weight that is below her natural set point.

Eating Disorders in Sports

The *Los Angeles Times* reported the following estimates of the prevalence of eating disorders in certain sports:[5]

Divers—Approximately 25 to 30 percent are either anorexic or bulimic.

Long-Distance Runners—Thirty-three percent of elite cross-country runners and 27 percent of elite long-distance runners suffer from eating disorders.

Tennis Players—Approximately 30 percent of the women on the pro tennis tour have some kind of eating disorder.

Swimmers—Of elite female swimmers between the ages of nine and eighteen, 70 percent were skipping meals to lose weight, nearly 70 percent had been told by their coaches to lose weight, and 41 percent thought they needed to lose weight to swim faster.

Gymnasts—Some 60 percent of female college gymnasts use dangerous methods of weight control. Of the gymnasts who performed poorly at the NCAA championships, over 80 percent were unhappy with their weight or eating habits.

By drastically cutting back on food intake at the same time that she pushes herself to excel physically, a girl or a young woman can develop a trio of interrelated disorders called the Female Athlete Triad. The triad begins with *disordered eating*, causing *amenorrhea* (loss of the menstrual period), which in turn can promote *osteoporosis* (the thinning of the bones). Untreated, these young women can end up in their twenties with bone densities equivalent to those of women in their seventies, a condition that may be permanent.

But just as coaches, trainers, and dance teachers can inadvertently help trigger eating disorders, they can also do much to prevent them. As a first step, all those who train or coach young people should learn about eating disorders, risk factors, and the signs of a disorder in progress. Once armed with this knowledge, they should:[6]

• Emphasize proper nutrition, especially during training and competition. Accurate information about weight, body composition, nutrition, and performance will reduce the myths and misinformation that trigger much disordered eating behavior.

• Discourage dangerous dieting or weight-control methods. Emphasize the health risks (such as amenorrhea and osteoporosis) associated with a too-low body weight.

• Teach athletes, students, and staff about the dangers of abnormally low body weight, dangerous weight-control methods, and poor nutrition.

• Emphasize performance rather than weight when assigning positions or roles or deciding who will and won't participate.

• Avoid group weigh-ins and making comments about weight.

• Be aware that younger athletes (especially those who enter national and international competitions) are at greater risk for developing eating disorders than older ones, since they're more vulnerable to the intense pressure. As famed women's gymnastics coach Bela Karolyi once said, "The young ones are the greatest little suckers in the world. They will follow you no matter what." (In recognition of this fact, the minimum age for unlimited international competition in gymnastics has recently been raised to sixteen; for professional tennis it's now eighteen.)

• Recognize signs of disordered eating in athletes/students and communicate concern. Take these warning signs seriously. Refer any athlete or dancer who is chronically dieting or seems to show signs of even mildly abnormal eating to a skilled eating disorders therapist. The sooner dangerous eating behaviors are treated, the better the outcome. Remember that severe eating disorders have a 10 to 15 percent mortality rate.

You, the coach/trainer/teacher, have tremendous power to influence your students. "Good" athletes are usually compliant ("coachable"), hardworking, highly motivated, and willing to do whatever it takes to achieve. What you say—right or wrong, positive or negative—can make an enormous impact, especially if you're dealing with young children. Use your power to guide young people toward health, happiness, and self-esteem as you guide them away from self-destructive attitudes and behaviors.

What do I do if my teenage daughter wants to diet?

First of all, you should explain to her that most diets don't work in the long run and that they can be dangerous, especially for a growing teenager. In *Child of Mine: Feeding with Love and Good Sense*, Ellyn Satter suggests that you vehemently resist your daughter's tendency to diet while agreeing that you will plan meals that are lower in fat and sugar. Don't start cooking special diet meals for her, though, because you'll be furious when she "falls off the wagon." Instead provide her with the nutritious foods that you give the rest of the family, ask her to join the family for all meals (hungry or not), and encourage her to take good care of her body.

If she still insists on dieting, stress "relaxed restraint." Cutting back slightly on portion sizes and staying away from calorie-dense foods are acceptable methods, unless they are taken too far. Remind her that eating too little food will lower her metabolic rate (making it likely that she'll *gain* weight), disturb proper functioning of her body (including female organs), sap her of energy, and possibly lead to eating disorders.

Henry Brooks Adams once said, "A teacher affects eternity; he can never tell where his influence stops." All of us—parents, teachers, coaches, family members, and others—are teachers and role models for the young people in our lives. With a little forethought, we can attack the problem of eating disorders at its root, and show them a better way to live.

Chapter Eight

WHAT YOU CAN DO TO HELP YOURSELF

The greatest discovery of any generation is that human beings can alter their lives by altering the attitudes of their minds.

—Albert Schweitzer

If you want to see bravery and persistence in action, watch a baby who's just learning to walk. She stands on her stout little legs, perhaps holding on to the edge of a coffee table, then lets go and takes her first wobbly little steps. She falls down, of course, but before you know it she's back up again, lurching off across the living room floor. You can help her by holding her hand or letting her hang on to a dish towel, but sooner or later she'll have to let go and do it herself.

Recovering from an eating disorder is a lot like learning to walk. Your family can lend a hand, your therapist can give you a dish towel to hang on to, your friends can urge you on from the sidelines, but in the end *you* will be the one taking those wobbly steps. Just as no one can force a baby to walk (she'll just sit down and let you drag her!), no one can force you to give up your eating disorder. *You* will have to decide that you want to become healthy again, *you* will have to commit yourself wholeheartedly to recovering, and *you* will have to do the work.

"You have to decide that you don't want your life ruled by an obsession. And food is one, whether you're gorging it or refusing it."[1]

—Ally Sheedy,
actress and former bulimic

What are some of the changes I'll need to make as I go through recovery?

Although your doctor, therapist, and dietitian will guide you down the road to recovery, there are several things that you can do to help yourself. They fall into three categories: *reducing your stress, changing your thinking,* and *changing your behavior*. You can begin doing some of these things right now, adding others as your recovery progresses. And just by reading through these suggestions and starting to think about them, you can take some positive steps toward reclaiming a healthy relationship with food.

What does reducing stress have to do with my eating disorder?

Stress, as you'll remember from Chapter 4, is a major component of the Cycle of Control. Defined in Merriam-Webster's dictionary as "mental tension" or "a constraining force or influence" (apropos for eating disorders!), stress can be the "straw that breaks the camel's back"— bringing on an episode of bingeing, purging, or further restriction of food. It makes sense, then, that reducing or releasing stress can make you less likely to get caught in the Cycle of Control.

How can I reduce the stress in my life?

First, you must learn to recognize the signs of stress. Although the stress that keeps an eating disorder "in business" is primarily mental or emotional, it often shows up in physical ways. Tightening of the jaw and face muscles, grinding of the teeth, tension in the neck and shoulders, or an upset stomach are just a few of the common physical symptoms of stress. Be on the lookout for the following signs:

Signs of Stress

- muscle tension
- fatigue
- teeth grinding or jaw clenching
- anxious feelings
- anger or irritability
- nervousness, shaking
- stomach upsets
- headache
- back pain
- weakness, dizziness

What's bugging you?

Once you recognize that you are indeed stressed, it's equally important to figure out what triggered it. To find out what's "bugging" you, make a conscious effort to tune in to your environment; pay attention to the people surrounding you, the daily scenarios you find yourself involved in, and the feelings that come up. As soon as you feel your jaw tightening or your stomach grinding, ask yourself, "What just happened to make me feel this way?"

You may wish to keep a Stress Log (see form in Appendix 1) in which you can write down what you're doing at certain times of the day, how you feel, and what your current stress level is. This can help you pinpoint the stress triggers and the times when you're most vulnerable. Here's an example from the Stress Log of a sixteen-year-old anorexic named Janet:

Date	Time	What Happened Immediately Before	Emotional State	Stress Symptoms	Stress-Relieving Technique Used
Mon. 8/8	9:10 A.M.	Weighing myself	I just feel so fat and angry with myself because I've gained a pound. It makes me never want to eat again	Headache	Took a warm bath

As you can see, Janet was feeling stressed in response to getting on the scale and seeing a slight weight gain. After thinking about it, Janet agreed that getting weighed *always* made her feel panicky, even when she'd lost weight. To relieve herself of some stress, she decided that she would throw away her scale and get weighed only when she visited her doctor.

Make it easy on yourself

Once you pinpoint something that stresses you, see if you can eliminate it. Carrie, a seventeen-year-old gymnast, found that gymnastic competitions were so stressful that she literally couldn't eat for days in advance. She finally decided that it wasn't worth it and stopped competing. She still does gymnastics, but only for fun. Darla realized that the biggest source of stress in her life was her stepmother. She moved in with her mother instead and now sees her father alone for dinner on Wednesdays and an outing on Saturdays. Alana's boss was so abusive and unpredictable that she found herself in a nervous state all day long, waiting for his next attack. She quit her job and went to work for someone who appreciated her. If you can change or eliminate the stressful situations in your life, by all means do so.

Defuse stress-making situations

Unfortunately we can't eliminate *all* the stressors in our lives. Meeting deadlines, taking tests, and fighting traffic, for example, are stressors that we just have to live with. But a little planning can do a lot to reduce their impact. For example, Brenda knew that she was going to have a big term paper due the same week that she was taking all of her final exams. Instead of waiting until the last few weeks of the term to start working on her paper, Brenda picked her topic and went to the library as soon as the teacher gave the assignment. She finished her paper a whole month in advance of the due date, then spent the rest of her time studying for finals. Brenda had effectively defused what could have been a stress bomb.

Elizabeth had to drive to and from work in heavy traffic five days a week. A trip that should have taken twenty-five minutes often stretched to fifty or sixty minutes as she inched her way down the freeway. By the time she reached her destination, she was often exhausted, angry, and stressed out. She knew she couldn't change the traffic or her work hours, so she decided to make the trip as pleasant as possible. She began checking out books on tape from the library. "That was the best thing I ever did for myself!" Elizabeth exclaimed. "Some days I'm so into the story that I don't want to get out of my car once I get to work. It really helps me to forget the aggravation of the freeway." Her "commuter's stress" had dwindled to nothing.

Defusing a stress-making situation can be as easy as getting up fifteen minutes earlier, doing a certain chore in the morning rather than at night, or tackling a project sooner rather than later. Using your Stress Log as a guide, consider the stress-making situations that you've faced in the last month. What can you do (rearrange your schedule, start earlier, provide a distraction, etc.) to help lessen or eliminate these stressors next time?

Remove yourself from situations that push "thinness"

If you're involved in a career, hobby, or group that is pushing you to attain some idealized body size (modeling, acting, cheerleading, dancing, athletics, etc.), either find a way to stay involved that doesn't threaten your health or consider giving it up. This may be painful, but if you don't, like Karen Carpenter and Christy Henrich, you could end up paying the ultimate price. No career or hobby is worth your life.

Christine Alt, sister of supermodel Carol Alt and a model herself, found herself in a life-threatening struggle to conform to the demands of her career. At 5'10½", Christine got down to 110 pounds and a size four dress by starving herself for an entire year on a diet of popcorn and one muffin a day. She had no energy, was irritable, developed an ulcer and a urinary tract problem, and fell into bingeing and purging. Her thinking became so distorted that when Karen Carpenter died of anorexia, all Christine could think was "God, she was so lucky that she died thin. How can I get to that point—being really thin without dying?"[2]

Eventually Christine realized that the price of staying in big-time fashion modeling was simply too great—she was a physical and emotional wreck. She returned to normal eating, and today at 155 pounds (which is the ideal weight for her height) Christine is a very successful "large-size" model. Her sister Carol says, "She looks wonderful. And she's so happy." By changing her thinking and her circumstances, Christine Alt managed to find a way to maintain both a thriving career and her health.

Ask yourself: Can I change the situation, or will the situation insist on changing me? If you can't change a situation that's threatening your health, then you need to ask yourself: Is staying involved in this career, hobby, or group *really* worth my health and sanity?

De-stress your life

Find ways to take the stress out of your life. As you think about your schedule, your obligations, and your commitments, ask yourself the following:

• Do you feel like you don't have time to do everything you're supposed to do? If so, you're probably trying to do too much. Try to lighten your load—take fewer classes, work fewer hours, or do less around the house if possible. Use the extra time to relax, meditate, listen to soothing music, or do other calming activities. *Don't* take on any more responsibilities or volunteer to do any more work.

• Is your life too fast-paced for comfort? Try slowing down a little. Walk, talk, and move more slowly than you normally would. Life isn't a race—you'll probably find that you can accomplish just as much without driving yourself so hard.

• Are you engaging in some form of relaxation every day? Don't neglect relaxation; it's essential to your health and well-being. (See relaxation tips below.)

• Are you feeling overly pressured at work? You may need to look for a new job. Don't let work compromise your health.

• Are you getting enough sleep? Most people need eight hours a night, some a little more, others a little less. Try to get *at least* seven every night.

• Is your body getting all the nutrients it needs? A healthful diet is a must for keeping stress at bay.

• Are you taking in too much caffeine? Caffeine can

"wire" you and make you a prime target for stress. Limit your caffeinated drinks to one or two a day. Better yet, try the decaffeinated forms of coffee, tea, or soft drinks.

• Are you exercising moderately? Experts generally recommend that we exercise three or four times a week for forty-five minutes to an hour. Adapt your activity to who you are and what you enjoy. The key is moderation—finding the middle ground between overdoing it and becoming a complete couch potato. Exercise should be an enjoyable experience that makes you feel good.

• Are you asking for help when you need it? Your therapist, doctor, dietitian, family, and friends are there for you. Reach out—you don't have to face your problems alone.

Find an escape valve

No matter how well we plan, no matter how "manageable" our lives may be, we all must live with a certain amount of stress. The trick is to find ways to release it before the stress seriously damages our bodies and minds. Just as a pressure cooker has a valve that releases steam a little at a time so the lid doesn't blow off, we need to find ways to release our own "steam."

When you're feeling stressed, find a healthy way to release the pressure as soon as possible. (You don't want to wait until you're so stressed that you want to tear your hair out!) There are a variety of specialists who can be very helpful to you in reducing anxiety. You might want to try massage therapy or acupuncture, for example. You can also use the following stress-releasing techniques throughout the day whenever you feel the need.

Stress-Releasing Activities
• Take a walk.
• Do some light exercise.

- Perform deep-breathing exercises.
- Take a warm bath.
- Listen to soothing music.
- Stretch.
- Practice yoga.
- Meditate.
- Daydream.
- Talk to a friend.
- Get a massage.
- Get back to nature—go to the mountains, the beach, or the country and just breathe the fresh air.

Finding ways to reduce the stress in your life will take some thinking and planning on your part, but it may be the easiest thing you can do to improve your health and mental outlook. More difficult but possibly even more important will be learning to change your thinking.

How can I change my thinking to help speed my recovery?

First, stop expecting so much of yourself. YOU HAVE THE RIGHT TO BE LESS THAN PERFECT. Indeed, *no one* is perfect, so we can all heave a big sigh of relief and forget about it! The sooner you realize that it's your right to *be yourself* instead of somebody's idealized image of perfection, the sooner you will be on the road to recovery.

Speaking of rights, people with eating disorders often forget (or never even realize) that they have certain rights simply because they're human beings. Once an eating disorder takes over a person's life, basic human rights tend to get trampled underfoot. So let's remind ourselves of our rights as human beings. Make a copy of these rights and hang them on your mirror as a daily reminder:

You Have the Right . . .

YOU HAVE THE RIGHT to be less than perfect.

YOU HAVE THE RIGHT to base your self-worth on inner qualities such as intelligence, creativity, generosity, and empathy instead of external qualities like weight, shape, or thinness.

YOU HAVE THE RIGHT to love yourself and receive love from others.

YOU HAVE THE RIGHT to be appreciated for the person that you are inside instead of the way you look.

YOU HAVE THE RIGHT to eat nourishing, appetizing foods in adequate amounts to restore and maintain your health.

YOU HAVE THE RIGHT not to be on a diet.

YOU HAVE THE RIGHT to rest when your body or mind gets tired.

YOU HAVE THE RIGHT to treat your body with respect and to refrain from dangerous or unhealthy practices.

YOU HAVE THE RIGHT to express your thoughts and feelings, whatever they may be.

YOU HAVE THE RIGHT to be listened to with respect and empathy.

YOU HAVE THE RIGHT to do things you enjoy, even if they call attention to your weight or shape.

YOU HAVE THE RIGHT to stop slave-driving yourself to attain some idealized image of perfection.

YOU HAVE THE RIGHT to wear clothes that appeal to you even if they call attention to your weight or shape.

YOU HAVE THE RIGHT to have friends.

YOU HAVE THE RIGHT to be free from verbal, physical, and sexual abuse.

YOU HAVE THE RIGHT to grow up and become a mature, fully functioning adult.

> YOU HAVE THE RIGHT to let others take
> responsibility for their own lives and actions.
>
> YOU HAVE THE RIGHT to pursue happiness while
> maintaining the right to be sad sometimes.
>
> YOU HAVE THE RIGHT to get professional help.
>
> YOU HAVE THE RIGHT to take all the time you need
> to recover.

As you progress toward recovery, your therapist and dietitian will help you gradually develop a completely different relationship with food. To do this you'll need to exchange many old, destructive behaviors for new, healthier ones. Since your behavior is determined by what you think, you'll need to throw out some of your old ideas and substitute new ones. You'll be doing this with the help of your treatment team. But you can really accelerate your recovery by adopting four simple ideas:

• *Forget dieting forever*—Dieting is the spark that sets off the eating disorder bonfire and keeps it going. If you're anorexic, your dieting has become so restrictive that your body is starving. If you're bulimic or a binge eater, your dieting is *causing* your cravings and binges. It also increases stress, anxiety, and feelings of failure, it lowers self-esteem, it fouls up hunger and satiety signals, and it brings on depression. Many people come to therapy to be cured of their eating disorders but still want to hold on to old dieting and weight-control methods. It's not possible. Your recovery will be stalled as long as you continue to try to control your body.

• *Tune in to your hunger and your fullness*—As you redefine your relationship with food, one of your most important tasks will be to learn to listen to your body's signals, especially those of hunger and fullness. After months or years of disordered eating behaviors, these signals will probably be somewhat out of whack, but as you begin to eat regular meals at regular times, they'll become more reliable. Gradually you and your body must relearn to eat in response to hunger rather than emotional issues. (Note: Until your hunger and fullness signals truly become reliable, your dietitian will probably ask you to follow a basic meal plan to make sure you're getting enough nutrients.)

• *Give yourself permission to eat*—Throw out your preconceived ideas of "good foods" and "bad foods," which foods will make you slim and which foods will make you fat. Instead decide what you *really want to eat*; then go ahead and have it. Don't make deals with yourself ("I can have this now, but only if I do 150 extra sit-ups tonight"). Instead, give yourself permission to eat.

You may think, "If I give myself permission to eat, I'll never stop. I'll eat everything in the house and gain fifty pounds!" Actually that's the furthest thing from the truth. When your body "knows" that its hunger signals will be respected, and your mind understands that you can have as much food as you want whenever you want it, that terrible urge to eat will disappear. You won't *need* to eat everything in the refrigerator, because you'll know that it will still be there next time you get hungry.

Think of a well-fed house cat and a cat roaming in the wild. If you put a bowl of food in front of each of them, the wild cat will gobble up every bite even if he's just eaten, because he never knows when he'll be able to eat again. But the house cat, who knows she'll be well fed every single day, can afford to turn her nose up at the food and wait until she's really hungry. Once you stop restricting food and start allowing yourself to eat, you'll find that your eating (like the house cat's) will be prompted by physical reasons ("I'm hungry") instead of psychological ones ("I'd better eat now because tomorrow I'm going on a really strict diet!").

• *Accept your body's natural weight and shape*—It's hard to develop a peaceful relationship with food when you're at war with your body's genetic blueprint. Bodies come in all shapes and sizes. Trying to force one body style to emulate another is always a recipe for disaster. You wouldn't expect your size ten feet to wear size five shoes, but you might well be trying to force your size ten body to fit into a size five dress. Accept the fact that bodies come in different sizes, just like feet. There is nothing wrong with having a large body, just as there is nothing wrong with having a small one.

Instead of thinking . . .	Think . . .
I need to diet . . .	I refuse to diet ever again.
I can have only 1/2 cup of this . . .	Am I hungry? If so, I'll eat until I feel full.
I'd better stop now, even though I'd like more . . .	Am I full? If so, I'll stop. If not, I'll keep eating.
That looks good, but I shouldn't eat it . . .	Do I really want it? If so, I'll eat it.
I hate my thighs!	My body looks the way nature intended it. This is the way a normal, healthy woman looks.
Am I too fat?	Am I healthy? If so, that's good enough.

Dumping the Diet

Jenny, a thirty-year-old office worker, had struggled to lose weight for years. She tried many different diets but found that they only made her want to eat more. "If the diet said 'eat one slice of bread,' I automatically wanted two," she says, sighing. "If it said 'three ounces of meat,' I had to have four. The harder I tried, the more my body fought me on it. Pretty soon I was bingeing, and then throwing up because I was so terrified of the calories.

"Finally one day I decided I was going to stop

dieting and start eating whatever I really wanted. I'd make an effort to eat healthy foods and try to feed my body well, but if I wanted a piece of chocolate cake, darn it, I'd go ahead and have it! I had three rules: 1) Eat when you're hungry; 2) Quit when you're full; and 3) If you really want something sweet or fatty or heavy, have it, but make sure you *really* want it. Six months after I started eating this way, I was stunned to see that my weight had stabilized at about eight pounds lower than it had been in years, and I had completely lost the urge to binge! I've stayed at this weight for a whole year now, and I don't work at it at all. I guess this must be my natural weight."

By reducing your stress levels and changing your thinking, changing your behavior should become a little easier.

What changes in behavior can I make to help my recovery?

Obviously, stopping the bingeing, purging, and/or food restrictions are the behavioral changes that you and your loved ones would like most to see. For most people, though, it's not just a matter of saying "Okay. I'll stop." It may be much more feasible to start making little changes in your behavior, which can help smooth the way for bigger changes. The following are some techniques you might find helpful:

• *Monitor your eating by keeping a Dietary Journal* (see Appendix 1 for the form)—Although this may seem like a cumbersome chore, it's important to keep a record of just what and how much you eat, where you are when eating, your emotional state at that time, whether or not you consider it a binge, and what (if any) compensating behaviors you use. A carefully kept Dietary Journal will help you pinpoint the emotional states, situations, foods, places, or times of day when you're most likely to have trouble. It will also help you be more specific in therapy when discussing your progress and setbacks.

• *Avoid "looksism"*—Make every effort to avoid judging people (including and especially yourself!) according to their looks. Get rid of your bathroom scale, spend as little time as possible looking in the mirror, throw out those extra-tight pants that you've been trying to fit into, and quit comparing your body with everyone else's. Above all, stop making those "body bashing" comments about yourself ("I hate my hips," "My arms are too flabby," etc.). Instead value yourself and others for what's on the inside.

• *Move your body just for the joy of it*—Instead of exercising to get rid of calories and fat, take a gentler approach. Walk, bike, skate, or jog at an easy pace just to feel the pleasant sensations as your muscles stretch and contract. Breathe deeply and enjoy the scenery; take it easy. Exercise should be energizing and stress relieving. It should be fun.

• *Treat your body with respect*—A good mother treats her baby's body with great respect. She understands that the baby needs (and deserves) to be fed, bathed, kept warm and dry, given adequate rest, cuddled, and loved. When the baby signals that she's hungry, the mother feeds her; when she sends signals that she's full, the mother stops. When the baby seems tired, she puts her to bed; when she wakes up, her mother picks her up and cuddles her. A good mother doesn't try to enforce her will upon her baby. Instead she responds to the baby's cues and interacts with her.

Think about the difference between the way you treat your body and the way a good mother would treat it. Would a good mother starve your body, force it to vomit, stuff it with laxatives, or insist that it exercise full bore for long periods of time? Would you do to your child (even if she was grown up) what you do to your own body? Start treating your body with the respect and tender, loving care of a good mother. You are your body's only caretaker. It depends on you to treat it right.

• *Validate yourself*—It's vitally important for all of us to get positive feedback about ourselves from both inside and outside. Take the time to sit down and make a list of at least ten positive things about yourself, focusing more on inner qualities than outer ones. Are you generous? A good listener? Intelligent? Creative? Write down as many positive attributes as you can, preceding each with the words "I am." Then when you're alone, read the list aloud, really letting the words sink in. By consistently reminding yourself that you are a worthwhile person with many positive traits, you will build a strong core of self-respect. Continue to add to the list over time (you may want to include positive comments you've received from others) and review the list at least once a day.

• *Repeat your affirmations*—An affirmation is a strong, positive statement about yourself that *you don't believe is true* but would like to be true. In fact, the less you believe it, the more power it may have. For example, you might tell yourself, "I can eat what I want and still feel good about myself," "I don't need to be thin to be happy," or "I love myself no matter what I weigh." Remember, the affirmation should reflect some aspect of your personality that you *wish* you had but don't believe that you do—yet.

How do I start using affirmations in my daily life?

Make a list of at least twenty affirmations; then pick a new one each day to repeat to yourself. Write it down on a slip of paper and carry it with you, or post it on your bathroom mirror. Then repeat it (aloud, if possible) ten times in the morning, ten times during the day, and ten times at night. Form a clear picture of it in your mind as you say it, and really feel it in your heart. One day you may be surprised to realize that it's no longer an affirmation, but a truth.

Try some of these or, better yet, make up your own:

- I am a positive, strong, capable person.
- I accept myself as I am—no matter how I look.
- I am good to myself.
- I treat my body with love and respect.
- I think highly of myself.
- I don't need to be thin to be happy.
- I love myself no matter what I weigh.
- What I think of myself does not depend on what others think of me.
- Although I might not always like what I do, I *always* like who I am.
- I eat only when I'm hungry, then stop when I'm full.
- I can completely change my old habits and routines.
- I am happy with my life.
- I can gain weight and still feel good about myself.
- I love myself even when I'm not perfect.
- I am a unique and lovable person.
- I take good care of myself.
- I can eat what I want and still feel good about myself.
- I am proud of myself and have nothing to be ashamed of.
- Every day I feel better and better.
- I am in control of my life.

- *Educate yourself*—Read, read, read all that you can about eating disorders. There are many excellent books, magazine articles, and videos on the subject of eating disorders (see Appendix 2). You can get plenty of literature on eating disorders from various organizations for free, or for a nominal fee. Knowledge is power—use it!

How can I help myself stop bingeing?

Bingeing is a problem that plagues not only bulimics and binge eaters but many anorexics as well. The most important thing that you can do to help yourself stop bingeing is to *eat satisfying meals at regular intervals throughout the day*. More often than not, binges are the result of overly restrictive eating. The most common example of this is the dieter who fasts or eats very little all day, then comes home at night and eats everything in sight. Her body, in effect, has "panicked" in response to a lack of food, and now sends out strong hunger signals. At the same time, it delays the feeling of fullness so that she can eat even more than usual. *If* she had eaten regularly throughout the day, however, she'd undoubtedly be eating much less at night.

A binge can be set in motion even if you've skipped only one meal (for example, breakfast), so make sure you always eat regular, healthful meals. Eating "regular meals" means eating breakfast, lunch, dinner, and usually two snacks—in the afternoon and at bedtime—*every day*. The sooner you being to eat "normally," the sooner you'll be able to break the bingeing cycle.

What is "normal" eating?

"Normal" eating is difficult to define precisely since it varies from individual to individual. (Normal eating for a 4'10" female office worker is very different from that of a 6'10" male basketball player.) Your dietitian will undoubtedly design a meal plan tailored to your needs. Still, it may be helpful to take a look at what's considered a normal, healthy eating pattern for the average person.

According to the Food Pyramid (the U.S. government guideline to healthy eating), the average person should be eating the following *as a minimum* every day:

- *Grains (bread, cereal, rice, pasta)—six servings:*
A half cup of cooked cereal, rice, or pasta or one slice of bread equals one grain serving. Grains are made up of complex carbohydrates, which provide your body with fuel, B vitamins, and fiber. Although carbohydrates may have a reputation for being "fattening," they are actually quite low in calories. Whole grains are preferable (whole wheat, rye, oats, brown rice, etc.).

- *Fruits/Vegetables—five servings:*
It's recommended that you eat two servings of fruit and three servings of vegetables daily. A serving consists of one cup of chopped raw vegetables or fruit, one medium-sized fruit, or a half cup of either vegetable or fruit juice. (Limit your juice servings to one a day, or you might not get enough fiber.) Fruits and vegetables supply beta-carotene (the plant form of vitamin A), vitamin C, folic acid, disease-fighting substances called phytochemicals, as well as fiber.

- *Protein (meat, poultry, fish, dried beans or peas, lentils, eggs)—two servings:*
A minimum serving of protein is two ounces of cooked meat, poultry, or fish; one cup of cooked beans, peas, or lentils; or one egg. Beans, peas, and lentils (a vitamin-rich, low-fat, high-fiber choice) should be eaten three times a week if possible. Protein is necessary for the growth and maintenance of body tissues; the production of hormones and enzymes; the maintenance of proper acid-base, fluid, and salt balances; and the manufacture of antibodies to fight off disease. We don't need a lot of protein, but we do require some.

- *Dairy (milk, yogurt, cheese)—two servings:*
Standard serving sizes are one cup of milk or yogurt, or

1¹/₂ ounces of cheese. The dairy group provides calcium, vitamin D, and protein, all of which are used for the growth and maintenance of the bones. Over time, a lack of calcium in the diet can lead to osteoporosis, a condition in which the bones become thin and brittle, fracturing easily.

- *Water—a half gallon or eight eight-ounce glasses per day*

Drinking plenty of water can help your system wash out toxins, prevent constipation, replenish fluids lost each day through normal metabolic processes, and reduce water retention or bloating. But to work effectively, water should be sipped a little at a time throughout the day. (Don't drink the whole half gallon at once—that's counterproductive!) Keep a bottle of water with you at all times to remind yourself to drink up.

The Food Pyramid system is not a diet. It is just a way to show the *minimum* number of servings of the food groups that we need each day. You will need *at least* this much food every day to maintain your health. Think of it as the framework of an eating plan; more food can be added according to individual needs and tastes, and you can (and should) vary your choices within the food groups. Also, when planning your meals, make sure you include some grains, some fruits or vegetables, and some protein at each meal. This is the best way to ensure that your blood sugar stays at a constant level (so you don't get too hungry or weak between meals), and a mix of foods actually helps the body absorb nutrients better.

If the Food Pyramid recommendations are too complicated to remember, try the Nutrition Countdown system[3] devised by Evelyn Tribole and Elyse Resch, authors of *Intuitive Eating*. To remember the minimum number of servings that you need each day, count backward from 6 to 1:

- 6 servings of Grains
- 5 servings of Fruits/Vegetables
- 4 ounces of Protein
- 3 servings of beans/peas/lentils **(per week)**
- 2 servings of Dairy
- 1 half gallon of water

So how does that break down into meals and snacks?

A general meal plan containing the minimum amount of foods the average person needs to maintain health might look something like this:

Breakfast

1 serving Grains	*(Translation*	1 piece of toast
1 serving Dairy	*into*	1 cup chocolate milk
1 serving Fruit	*real food:)*	1 pear, sliced

Lunch

2 servings Grains	1 tuna sandwich
1 serving Protein	(2 pieces of bread/2 oz. tuna)
1 serving Vegetables	Mixed vegetable salad

Snack

1 serving Grains	4 whole wheat crackers
1 serving Vegetables	1 cup carrot sticks

Dinner

2 servings Grains	1 cup pasta
1 serving Protein	Spaghetti sauce w/2 oz. meat
1 serving Vegetables	1/2 cup cooked zucchini

Snack

1 serving Fruit	1/2 cantaloupe
1 serving Dairy	1 cup yogurt

This meal plan is only included to give you a general idea of the bare bones of "normal, healthy eating," as well as to illustrate that a normal meal or snack is *not* just a lettuce leaf and a glass of iced tea. It's important to note that this may *not* be a good meal plan for you. If you've gotten used to eating practically nothing and are just beginning to eat again, this could be far too much to start with. On the other hand, if you're a binge eater, this won't be nearly enough to satisfy you. Those who need to gain weight will also need to eat more. To find out exactly what *you* should be eating, confer with your dietitian.

What if I'm not hungry or don't feel like eating a particular food? Should I ignore my body's signals and eat it anyway?

When you're just beginning to eat normally again, you will probably have to stick to the meal plan as you gradually learn to read your body's signals. The trouble with relying on bodily signals early in the refeeding process is that they have been scrambled by your eating disorder. Tuning in to hunger and fullness is a more subtle skill that you'll acquire with time and practice as your body regains health and strength. *The most important thing is to feed your body properly and regularly.* If you're truly not hungry, you might delay your meal thirty to sixty minutes. But under no circumstances should you skip a meal or delay it for more than one hour. Remember: *Skipped or long-delayed meals set you up for bingeing.*

What else can I do to prevent bingeing?

Besides eating regularly, you can help prevent bingeing by doing the following:

• *Identify triggers*—Review your Stress Log or your Dietary Journal to pinpoint the emotions, situations, or activities that make you feel like bingeing. Is it stress, anxiety, anger, or depression? Is it boredom, loneliness, or exhaustion? Perhaps cooking sets you off, or going to parties, or arguing with your mother. Maybe having certain foods in the house is a trigger, or having too much unscheduled time alone. Try to be as specific as possible when identifying the things that trigger your binges.

• *Plan ahead*—Once you can determine what your triggers are, you'll be in a much better position to plan strategies for avoiding, altering, or dealing with these things. The strategies differ for each person, but you may want to consider some of these ideas:

• Make your meals enjoyable, relaxing, sensual events. Really see, smell, and taste your food. Eat slowly and savor the flavors. Don't eat standing up or while reading, watching TV, or engaging in any other activities. Eat with others who are good company and will engage in pleasant conversation.

• Plan your meals and snacks the day before to relieve yourself of last-minute stress.

• If you binge as you unload groceries after shopping, try to get someone else to do it for you—or at least be with you while you're doing the unloading.

• Plan to get involved in an enjoyable activity immediately after your meal so that you won't be tempted to continue eating.

• Enjoy a variety of foods. Eating the same foods over and over leads to boredom and black-and-white thinking (This food is "good," this one is "bad").

• Bring healthful snacks with you when you're out so that you won't be faced with the choice of either eating "trigger" foods or eating nothing at all.

• Get out of the house as much as possible during the times you normally binge. Take a class, go visit a friend, see a movie. Do whatever you can to ensure that you're not alone during your vulnerable times.

• *Reach out to others*—The support that you get from friends and family can be invaluable to you as you fight your way back to recovery. Set up a support system for yourself consisting of a few caring, encouraging, trustworthy people who understand your condition and are willing to be there for you. Then use them! Stay in close contact, keep them informed of your progress, and ask for help when you need it. Your support system can help you continue to fight, especially when you feel like you can't go on any longer.

• *Avoid alcohol and recreational drugs*—Alcohol and recreational drugs alter your perception and undermine your self-control. Obviously these are the *last* things you need when you're trying to reshape your thinking and tackle emotional problems. Suffice it to say, using these substances will set your progress back substantially.

What do I do if I feel like bingeing *right now*?

First, realize that you *can* intervene; you don't have to give in to the urge! Many bingers mistakenly believe that once they get the urge to binge, it will continue to plague them, growing increasingly stronger until they finally surrender. In fact, the opposite is true. The longer you can put off bingeing, the weaker the impulse will become. And the more times you successfully withstand the urge to binge, the *less* often the urge will arise. You'll also find that it becomes easier and easier to withstand bingeing.

To intervene when you feel like bingeing, try the following:

• Leave the binge environment immediately. Take a walk or a drive, ride a bike, go to the movies, or go shopping. Once you're out of the environment, you may find that the urge to binge disappears.

• Ask yourself, "Is this really worth bingeing over?"

• Find someone to spend time with. If you're like most bingers, you binge in secret when you're alone, and you are much less likely to do so when you've got company. Make sure that the two of you engage in nonfood activities, though. Two bingers can end up egging each other on.

• If you can't physically be with someone, call a friend who understands what you're going through and will listen. Keep talking until the urge passes.

• Practice the stress-releasing activities listed earlier. Do deep breathing or yoga, meditate, listen to soothing music, or get a massage. Most binges are brought on by anxiety and stress, so anything you can do to relieve these conditions may help you stay in control.

• In your journal, write down exactly what you're feeling, where you are, and all the circumstances surrounding your urge to binge. Note the intervention techniques that you're currently using. This will help you determine what works and what doesn't for next time.

• Do something that keeps your hands busy, such as sewing, knitting, gardening, painting, or playing a musical instrument. These activities are much more likely to block out thoughts of food than the more passive ones like reading or watching TV.

• Take a long, hot scented bath.

• Repeat your affirmations.

What if I wind up bingeing anyway?

If you do binge, realize that it's *not* the end of the world. You will have setbacks on the road to recovery, and many times they'll offer you some of your best learning opportunities. Do some detective work by reviewing what you've written in your Dietary Journal or Stress Log, looking for clues. What were the feelings, circumstances, or outside influences that helped bring on the binge? What can you do to prevent or change these circumstances for next time? How can you alter your own actions so you don't get caught in the Cycle of Control? Your logs and journals can provide great insight into the causes of your eating disorder *if* you really tune in to yourself and your surroundings and make careful, consistent notes.

So let's say that you're eating regular, healthful meals and using prevention techniques, but the urge to binge strikes anyway. You try several interventions and manage to put it off for a while, but finally you give in and binge. Don't sweat it. Just putting off the binge is progress. Next time you'll be able to put it off longer, or maybe altogether. *Just make sure that you don't purge.*

It's vitally important to remember that *purging* is the mechanism that keeps the bulimic cycle in motion. If and when you binge, *strongly resist the impulse to purge*. Once you stop purging, your binges will gradually taper off. As long as you continue to purge, however, you will remain caught in the cycle. The same intervention techniques that are useful for stopping a binge can be used to help you resist the "urge to purge."

What if I end up purging anyway?

Once again, you must remind yourself that your life is not over just because you've had a setback. Leave the guilt and self-loathing behind while you try to figure out what happened and why. Then plan accordingly for next time. You certainly won't win every battle in your war against eating disorders, but you *can* fight your way back to health if you refuse to give up!

Things You Can Do to Help Yourself

To Reduce Stress:

- Keep a Stress Log.
- Eliminate stressors.
- Defuse stress-making situations.
- Slow down.
- Don't overdo it.
- Use stress-releasing techniques.
- Consume a healthy diet.
- Exercise moderately.
- Remove yourself from situations that push thinness.
- Ask for help.

To Change Your Thinking:

- Realize that you don't have to be perfect.
- Read your "Rights" daily.
- Forget dieting forever.
- Tune in to hunger and satiety.
- Give yourself permission to eat.
- Accept your body's natural weight and shape.

To Change Your Behavior:

- Keep a Dietary Journal.
- Avoid looksism.
- Move your body just for the joy of it.
- Treat your body with respect.
- Validate yourself.
- Repeat your affirmations.
- Educate yourself.

To Prevent Bingeing:

- Eat satisfying meals at regular intervals.
- Identify triggers.
- Plan ahead.
- Reach out to others.
- Avoid alcohol and recreational drugs.
- Avoid purging, even if you do binge.

To Intervene During a Binge:

- Leave the binge environment.
- Find someone to spend time with.
- Practice stress-releasing techniques.
- Keep your hands busy.
- Repeat your affirmations.
- Call your therapist.

Remember the baby at the beginning of the chapter who was just learning to walk? Every time she took a step, she fell down—but she doggedly got back up and tried again, over and over. Lo and behold, one day she took off *running*. Your recovery will have similar fits and starts, but you can make it if you keep trying.

Appendix 1

EATING DISORDER
WORKBOOK

The forms, questionnaires, and exercises in this section are designed to make you more aware of what sets off your eating disorder, what you can do to intervene, and how positive self-talk can turn your life around. *They are not meant to replace your therapy!* Use them as an adjunct to therapy and a way to keep yourself on track. (Note: Some people will find these forms, questionnaires, and exercises useful; others won't. It's up to you.)

Remember that recovering from an eating disorder doesn't just happen—it takes a great deal of time, commitment, and hard work. Sometimes it will be very difficult, scary, and uncomfortable. But the peace and serenity of a life free from food and weight obsessions are well worth the effort.

DIETARY JOURNAL

Using the following as a guide, keep a record of what you eat, how you're feeling emotionally at the time, how hungry you are, whether or not you end up bingeing, and what you do to compensate for that binge (if anything). The Dietary Journal can help you pinpoint just what triggers your eating behaviors, making you more aware of what you're doing and why. It can be an important tool, but only if you use it! Scrupulously enter every single thing you eat (even one bite!) and tune in to your feelings. The more you put into this journal, the more you'll get out of it.

Date:

Time	Place	Foods Eaten/ Amount	How You Felt Emotionally Before Eating	Scale of Hunger (0–4)	Do You Consider This a Binge?	Compensating Behavior?	How Did You Feel After Episode?
Example: 8:00 P.M.	Home	½ gallon ice cream	Depressed, nervous	2	Yes	Threw up	Disgusted, depressed

If You've Binged. . .

If, in spite of your best efforts, you end up bingeing, realize that it's *not* the end of the world. It's a temporary setback but also a great opportunity to learn about yourself. Check back over your Dietary Journal and your Stress Log and answer the following questions:

1. What do you think triggered the binge? (circumstances, outside influences, feelings, etc.)

_____
_____
_____
_____
_____
_____

2. What can you do to prevent the same thing from happening again?

_____
_____
_____
_____
_____
_____

3. How can you change your own actions next time so you don't get caught in the Cycle of Control?

_____
_____
_____
_____
_____
_____

STRESS LOG

The Stress Log is similar to the Dietary Journal, but here you're trying to determine what makes you anxious, fearful, irritable, or depressed. It isn't enough to say that "food" or "not being thin enough" brings on these emotional states. They're just symptoms of greater conflicts inside.

For a revealing look at "what's bugging you," every time you feel tense, nervous, shaky, sick to your stomach, or headachy, make a note of it in your Stress Log. Be sure to note how you were feeling emotionally at the time (angry, depressed, etc.) and which stress-relieving techniques you used (medication, warm bath, relaxation tapes, bingeing, purging, etc.).

Date	Time	What Happened Immediately Before	Stress Symptoms	Emotional State	Stress-Relieving Techniques Used
Example: 8/8	4:00 P.M.	Got into argument with my mother	Nervous, shaky, sick to my stomach	Anxious, fearful, angry	Tried to meditate; ended up eating three raw carrots really fast. I wanted to _crunch_ on something.

Stress-Making Situations

Review your Stress Log and pick out five situations during which you felt the most stressed. It could be when your dog ran away, you got a bad grade on a test, your mother yelled at you for losing too much weight, etc. List the five situations in the spaces below.

Below each situation, write: a) Three things you did (or could have done) to handle the stress; and b) Three things you can do to prevent the same situation from occurring again.

<u>Example:</u>

Stress-Making Situation: I was caught shoplifting candy in the grocery store.

Three Ways to Handle the Stress (after making amends with the shopkeeper):
1. Do deep-breathing exercises.
2. Take a warm bath.
3. Practice relaxation techniques.

To Prevent Same Situation from Happening Again:
1. Talk to my therapist to discover why I shoplifted.
2. Eat regular, healthful meals so I won't be overly hungry.
3. Always shop with someone else.

STRESS-MAKING SITUATION #1:

_____
_____
_____

Three Ways to Handle the Stress:
1. _____
2. _____
3. _____

To Prevent Same Situation from Happening Again:
1. _____
2. _____
3. _____

STRESS-MAKING SITUATION #2:

_____

_____

_____

Three Ways to Handle the Stress:
1. _____
2. _____
3. _____

To Prevent Same Situation from Happening Again:
1. _____
2. _____
3. _____

STRESS-MAKING SITUATION #3:

_____

_____

_____

Three Ways to Handle the Stress:
1. _____
2. _____
3. _____

To Prevent Same Situation from Happening Again:
1. _____
2. _____
3. _____

STRESS-MAKING SITUATION #4:
1. _____
2. _____
3. _____

Three Ways to Handle the Stress:
1. _____
2. _____
3. _____

To Prevent Same Situation from Happening Again:
1. _____
2. _____
3. _____

STRESS-MAKING SITUATION #5:
1. _____
2. _____
3. _____

Three Ways to Handle the Stress:
1. _____
2. _____
3. _____

To Prevent Same Situation from Happening Again:
1. _____
2. _____
3. _____

Validate Yourself

It's vitally important for all of us to get positive feedback about ourselves from both inside and outside. Make a list of at least ten positive things about yourself, focusing more on inner qualities than outer ones. Are you generous? Are you a good listener? Are you intelligent? Are you creative? Write down as many positive attributes as you can, preceding each with the words "I am." Then when you're alone, read the list aloud and really let the words sink in.

Over time, continue to add to the list. You may want to include positive comments you've received from others. Review the list at least once a day.

1. I am _____
2. I am _____
3. I am _____
4. I am _____
5. I am _____

6.   I am _____
7.   I am _____
8.   I am _____
9.   I am _____
10. I am _____

Affirmations

An affirmation is a strong, positive statement about yourself that *you don't believe is true* but would like to be true. In fact, the less you believe it, the more power it may have. For example, you might tell yourself, "I can eat what I want and still feel good about myself," "I don't need to be thin to be happy," or "I love myself no matter what I weigh." Remember, it should reflect some aspect of your personality that you *wish* you had but don't believe that you do—yet.

Make a list of at least twenty affirmations. You can use some of the examples below if you like them or, better yet, make up some of your own.

Examples:

- I am a positive, strong, capable person.
- I accept myself as I am—no matter how I look.
- I am good to myself.
- I treat my body with love and respect.
- I think highly of myself.
- I don't need to be thin to be happy.
- I love myself no matter what I weigh.
- What I think of myself does not depend on what others think of me.
- Although I might not always like what I do, I *always* like who I am.
- I eat only when I'm hungry and then stop when I'm full.
- I can completely change my old habits and routines.
- I am happy with my life.

- I can gain weight and still feel good about myself.
- I love myself even when I'm not perfect.
- I am a unique and lovable person.
- I take good care of myself.
- I can eat what I want and still feel good about myself.
- I am proud of myself and have nothing to be ashamed of.
- Every day I feel better and better.
- I am in control of my life.

MY AFFIRMATIONS

1. _____
2. _____
3. _____
4. _____
5. _____
6. _____
7. _____
8. _____
9. _____
10. _____
11. _____
12. _____
13. _____
14. _____
15. _____
16. _____
17. _____
18. _____
19. _____
20. _____

Each morning pick a different affirmation and repeat it ten times in the morning, ten times during the day, and ten times at night. Write it down on a slip of paper so you can carry it with you, or post it on your bathroom mirror. Form a clear picture of the affirmation in your mind as you say it, and really feel it in your heart. Eventually they'll stop being affirmations—they'll be the truth.

Getting What You Need

For many of us, one of the hardest things to do is to *ask* for what we need. We're afraid of rejection; we're afraid we're not worthy; we're afraid we'll look helpless and vulnerable. But if you begin with the belief that you're a lovable, worthy person, asking becomes easier. Tell yourself, "My needs are important because I am a worthwhile person. Even though I risk rejection, I'm going to ask for what I need."

To help you learn to ask for what you need, answer the following questions:

1. What do you do right now when you need to ask for something?
  a) I don't ask.
  b) I'd have to really, really need it before I'd ask.
  c) I think those around me should realize that I need it before I ask.
  d) I'll ask, but only if I'm 99 percent sure that I'll be told yes.
  e) I ask freely, without worrying about it.

2. List four things that you *haven't* asked for recently, even though you may really have wanted or needed them. (Look for clues in your diaries and logs.)
1. _____
2. _____
3. _____
4. _____

3. Name four changes in your life that you would like to ask for (for example, more privacy, lots of listening, more affection).

1. _____

2. _____

3. _____

4. _____

4. Of the four things you listed in question #3, pick one to ask for. Fill in the blanks: I'm going to ask for _____ from _____.

I think the response will be _____. *(Now ask!)*

I felt _____ when I asked.

The response was _____.

Appendix 2
WHERE TO FIND HELP

ORGANIZATIONS–UNITED STATES

Ackerman Institute for the Family
149 E. 78th Street
New York, NY 10021
Phone: (212) 879-4900
(Provides family therapy)

AA/BA (American Anorexia/Bulimia Association)
c/o Regent Hospital
293 Central Park West, Ste. 1R
New York, NY 10024
Phone: (212) 501-8351
(Provides educational material on eating disorders and their
treatment and prevention. Also sponsors support groups, puts
out a newsletter, and has a hot line Monday through Friday
9:00 A.M. to 5:00 P.M. Will give referrals over the phone.)

**ANAD (National Association of Anorexia
Nervosa & Related Disorders)**
Box 7
Highland Park, IL 60035
Phone: (708) 831-3438
(Provides information on support groups, an international
listing of hospitals and therapists, and a crisis hot line.
Monday through Friday 9:00 A.M. to 5:00 P.M.)

ANRED (Anorexia Nervosa & Related Eating Disorders Inc.)
Box 5102
Eugene, OR 97405

Phone: (541) 344-1144
(Provides national and some international referrals, a
newsletter, educational brochures, and information on
starting a support group.)

**EDAP (Eating Disorders Awareness
and Prevention)**
603 Stewart St., Ste. 803
Seattle, WA 98101
Phone: (206) 382-3587
(Provides educational materials to schools, health
professionals, community organizations, and individuals.
Sponsors Eating Disorders Awareness Week and a puppet
project for schools.)

EDRC (Eating Disorder Resource Center)
24 E. 12th St., Ste. 505
New York, NY 10003
Phone: (212) 989-3987
(Outpatient center offering individual, group, and family
treatment.)

**MEDA (Massachusetts Eating Disorders
Association)**
1162 Beacon St.
Brookline, MA 02146
Phone: (617) 738-6332
(Provides support line, educational information, treatment
referrals, and a newsletter.)

**NAAFA (National Association to Advance
Fat Acceptance)**
P.O. Box 188620
Sacramento, CA 95188
Phone: (916) 558-6880
(Provides a newsletter and educational information; sponsors
a national conference.)

NEDO (National Eating Disorders Organization)
6655 South Yale Ave.
Tulsa, OK 74136
Phone: (918) 481-4044 (Mon.–Fri.)
(Provides educational information and has International Treatment Referral Directory with over 900 resources, a Support Group Registry, a newsletter, and information on how to develop your own support group.)

NIMH (National Institute of Mental Health)
Information Resources and Inquiries Branch
5600 Fishers Lane, Rm. 7C-02
Bethesda, MD 20857
Phone: (301) 443-4513
(Provides brochure on eating disorders.)

ORGANIZATIONS—OUTSIDE THE UNITED STATES

Australia

The Anorexia and Bulimia Nervosa Foundation
1513 High St.
Glen Iris
3146 Victoria
Australia
Phone: (613) 885-0318

Canada

Anti-Anorexia/Anti-Bulimia League
207-1168 Hamilton St.
Vancouver, BC
Canada V6B 252
Phone: (604) 688-7860

Bulimia Anorexia Nervosa Association
c/o Psychological Service
University of Windsor
Ontario
Canada N9B 3PH
Phone: (519) 253-7421 or (519) 253-7545

The National Eating Disorders Information Center
CW-134
200 Elizabeth St.
Toronto, Ontario
Canada M5G 2C4
Phone: (416) 340-4156
(Provides educational information; sponsors Eating Disorders
Awareness Week in Canada.)

Great Britain

The Eating Disorders Association
Sackville Pl.
44 Magdalen St.
Norwich, UK
Phone: (01603) 621414

New Zealand

Women with Eating Disorders Resource Centre
P.O. Box 4520
Armagh and Montreal St.
Christchurch, New Zealand
Phone: (643) 366-7725

JOURNALS AND NEWSLETTERS

AABA (American Anorexia/Bulimia Association)
(See address above.)

ANRED (Anorexia Nervosa & Related Eating Disorders Inc.)
(See address above.)

Eating Disorders: The Journal of Treatment and Prevention
New York: Bruner Mazel
Leigh Cohn, Editor
(A quarterly publication.)

Healthy Weight Journal
402 South 14th St.
Hettinger, ND 58639
Phone: (701) 567-2646
(National newsletter and information.)

International Journal of Eating Disorders
New York: John Wiley & Sons
Michael Strober, Editor
(A quarterly publication.)

MEDA (Massachusetts Eating Disorders Association)
(See address above.)

NAAFA (National Association to Advance Fat Acceptance)
(See address above.)

NEDO (National Eating Disorders Organization)
(See address above.)

RECOMMENDED READING

Am I Thin Enough Yet? The Cult of Thinness and the Commercialization of Identity
Hesse-Biber, Sharlene. New York: Oxford University Press, 1996.

Anorexia and Bulimia: Anatomy of a Social Epidemic
Gordon, Richard A. Cambridge, Mass.: Blackwell, 1995.

The Beauty Myth
Wolf, Naomi. New York: William Morrow, 1991.

Beyond the Food Game: A Spiritual and Psychological Approach to Healing Emotional Eating
Latimer, Jane. Denver: LivingQuest, 1993.

The Body Betrayed: A Deeper Understanding of Women, Eating Disorders, and Treatment
Zerbe, Katherine. Washington, D.C., London: American Psychiatric Press, 1993.

Breaking Free from Compulsive Eating
Roth, Geneen. New York: Plume Books (Penguin), 1984.

Bulimia: A Guide to Recovery
Hall, Lindsey, and Leigh Cohn. Carlsbad, Calif: Gurze Books, 1992.

Bulimia Nervosa and Binge-Eating: A Guide to Recovery
Cooper, Peter J. New York: New York University Press, 1996.

Compulsive Overeating
Bill, B. Center City, Minn: Hazelden, 1981.

The Deadly Diet, 2nd ed.
Sandbek, Terence J. Oakland, Calif: New Harbinger Publications, Inc., 1993.

The Eating Disorder Sourcebook
Costin, Carolyn. Los Angeles: Lowell House, 1996.

Eating Disorders
Bruch, Hilde. New York: Basic Books, 1973.

Eating Disorders Book Catalogue (free)
Gurze Books
Box 2238
Carlsbad, CA 92018
Phone: (800) 756-7533

Eating Disorders: Nutrition Therapy in the Recovery Process
Reiff, D. W., and K. K. Reiff. Aspen, Md.: Aspen Publishers, 1992.

Eating Disorders: Obesity, Anorexia and the Person Within
Bruch, Hilde. New York: Basic Books, 1973.

Father Hunger: Fathers, Daughters and Food
Maine, Margo. Carlsbad, Calif.: Gurze Books, 1991.

Fat Is a Feminist Issue
Orbach, Susie. New York: Paddington Press; Berkeley Medallion Books, 1978.

Feminist Perspectives on Eating Disorders
Fallon, Patricia, et al. New York: Guilford Press, 1994.

Full Lives: Women Who Have Freed Themselves from Food and Weight Obsessions
Hall, Lindsey. Carlsbad, Calif.: Gurze Books, 1993.

The Golden Cage: The Enigma of Anorexia Nervosa
Bruch, Hilde. Cambridge, Mass.: Harvard University Press, 1978.

Hope, Help & Healing for Eating Disorders
Jantz, Gregory L. Wheaton, Ill.: Harold Shaw Publishers, 1995.

Hunger Pains: The Modern Woman's Tragic Quest for Thinness
Pipher, Mary. New York: Ballantine Books, 1995.

Intuitive Eating: A Recovery Book for the Chronic Dieter
Tribole, Evelyn, and Elyse Resch. New York: St. Martin's Press, 1995.

The Invisible Woman: Confronting Weight Prejudice in America
Goodman, W. Charisse. Carlsbad, Calif.: Gurze Books, 1997.

Living Binge Free
Latimer, Jane. Denver: LivingQuest, 1988.

Losing It: America's Obsession with Weight and the Industry That Feeds on It
Fraser, Laura. New York: Dutton Books, 1997.

Making Peace with Food
Kano, Susan. New York: Harper & Row, 1989.

Mothering Ourselves
Bassoff, Evelyn: New York: Plume, 1992.

The Obsession: Reflections on the Tyranny of Slenderness
Chernin, Kim. New York: Harper & Row, 1981.

Overcoming Addictions
Chopra, Deepak. New York: Harmony Books, 1997.

Overcoming Binge Eating
Fairburn, Christopher. New York: The Guilford Press, 1995.

Overcoming Overeating
Munter, Carol, and Jane R. Hirschmann. Reading, Mass.: Addison-Wesley, 1988.

Treating and Overcoming Anorexia Nervosa
Levenkron, Steven. New York: Scribner's, 1982.

When Food Is Love: Exploring the Relationships Between Intimacy and Eating
Roth, Geneen. New York: Dutton, 1991.

When Women Stop Hating Their Bodies
Hirschmann, Jane, and Carol Munter. New York: Fawcett, 1995.

BOOKS FOR FAMILIES AND FRIENDS

Bulimia: A Guide for Family and Friends
Sherman, R. T., and R. A. Thompson. Lexington, Mass.: Lexington Books, 1990.

Fasting Girls: The Emergence of Anorexia Nervosa as a Modern Disease
Brumberg, J. Cambridge, Mass.: Harvard University Press, 1988.

How to Get Your Kid to Eat . . . But Not Too Much
Satter, Ellyn. Palo Alto, Calif.: Bull Publishing Co., 1987.

Like Mother, Like Daughter
Waterhouse, Deborah. New York: Hyperion, 1997.

A Parent's Guide to Anorexia and Bulimia
Byrne, Katherine. New York: Henry Holt, 1987.

Reviving Ophelia: Saving the Selves of Adolescent Girls
Pipher, Mary. New York: Ballantine Books, 1994.

Surviving an Eating Disorder: Strategies for Family and Friends—Revised and Updated
Siegel, Michele, Judith Brisman, and Margot Weinshel. New York: HarperCollins, 1997.

When Will We Laugh Again? Living and Dealing with Anorexia Nervosa and Bulimia
Kinoy, Barbara, Estelle Miller, John Atchley, and the Book Committee of the American Anorexia/Bulimia Association. New York: Columbia University Press, 1984.

Your Dieting Daughter
Costin, Carolyn. New York: Brunner Mazel, 1996.

BOOKS FOR CHILDREN
(FOR EATING DISORDERS AWARENESS AND
PREVENTION)

Blubber
Blume, Judy. New York: Bantam Doubleday Dell Publishing Group, 1974.

Good Answers to Tough Questions About Weight Problems and Eating
Berry, Joy. Chicago: Children's Press, 1990.

Heads You Win, Tails I Lose
Holland, Isabelle. New York: Ballantine Books, 1973.

Nothing's Fair in Fifth Grade
DeClements, Barthe. New York: Penguin Books, 1990.

One Fat Summer
Lipsyte, Robert. New York: HarperCollins, 1977.

The Pig-Out Blues
Greenberg, Jan. New York: Farrar, Straus & Giroux, 1982.

Tales of a Fourth Grade Nothing
Blume, Judy. New York: Bantam Doubleday Dell Publishing Group, 1972.

VIDEOS

(These videos are available for sale from the companies indicated. Company addresses and phone numbers are listed at the end of this section.)

Anorexia and Bulimia (19 min.)—Films for the Humanities & Sciences

Anorexia Nervosa: The Covert Rebellion (26 min.)—Aims Media

An Anorexic's Tale: The Brief Life of Catherine (80 min.)—Films for the Humanities & Sciences

Beyond the Looking Glass: Self-Esteem and Body Image (28 min.)—HRM Video

Bulimia: The Binge/Purge Syndrome (20 min.)—Aims Media

Bulimia: Out-of-Control Eating (23 min.)—Aims Media

Eating Disorders (26 min.)—Films for the Humanities & Sciences

Eating Disorders: Myths vs. Realities (30 min.)—Therapeutic Education

Eating Disorders: The Slender Trap (21 min.)—Aims Media

Faces of Recovery (35 min.)—Gurze Books

The Famine Within (90 min.)—Direct Cinema Ltd.

Feeling Good About Me (15 min.)—Sunburst Communications

Foodfright (30 min.)—Direct Cinema Ltd.

In Our Own Words: Personal Accounts of Eating Disorders (30 min.)—EDAP

Mirror, Mirror (14 min.)—UCSB

The Perfect Body (14 min.)—UCSB

Pregnancy and Eating Disorders (28 min.)—Films for the Humanities & Sciences

Real People: Coping with Eating Disorders (27 min.)—Sunburst Communications

A Season in Hell (59 min.)—New Day Films

The Secret Life of Mary-Margaret: Portrait of a Bulimic (30 min.)—Aims Media

Skin Deep (26 min.)—Disney Educational Productions

Slim Hopes (30 min.)—Media Education

Still Killing Us Softly (30 min.)—Cambridge Films

When Food Is an Obsession: Overcoming Eating Disorders (28 min.)—HRM Video

Video Companies

Aims Media
9710 DeSoto Ave.
Chatsworth, CA 91311
Phone: (800) 367-2467

Cambridge Films
P.O. Box 385
Cambridge, MA 02139
Phone: (617) 354-3677

Direct Cinema Ltd.
P.O. Box 10003
Santa Monica, CA 90410
Phone: (800) 525-0000

Disney Educational Productions
105 Terry Dr., Ste. 120
Newtown, PA 18940
Phone: (800) 295-5010

EDAP
603 Stewart St., Ste. 803
Seattle, WA 98101
Phone: (206) 382-3587

Films for the Humanities & Sciences
P.O. Box 2053
Princeton, NJ 08543
Phone: (800) 257-5126

Gurze Books
P.O. Box 2238
Carlsbad, CA 92018-9883
Phone: (800) 756-7533

HRM Video
175 Tompkins Ave.
Pleasantville, NY 10570
Phone: (800) 431-2050

Media Education
26 Center St.
Northampton, MA 01060
Phone: (800) 659-6882

New Day Films
22-D Hollywood Ave.
Hohokus, NJ 07423
Phone: (201) 652-6590

Sunburst Communications
39 Washington Ave.
Pleasantville, NY 10570
Phone: (800) 431-1934

Therapeutic Education
514 S. Livingston Ave.
Livingston, NJ 07032
Phone: (201) 740-9085

UCSB
Student Health Service
Health Education Dept.
Santa Barbara, CA 93106
Phone: (805) 893-2086

TREATMENT CENTERS

There are many treatment centers scattered around the country. You can look for such centers in your community by calling local hospitals, medical schools, and mental health clinics.

The following are just a few of the treatment centers offering inpatient, partial day (after school or work), residential (live-in, but not in a hospital), or outpatient programs. Each listing indicates the programs offered: Inpatient (I), Partial Day (P), Residential (R), and Outpatient (O).

Bethesda Psychiatric Health Center (I, P)
4400 East Cliff Ave.
Denver, CO 80222
Phone: (303) 758-6195

Columbia Presbyterian Hospital (O, I)

722 West 168th St.
New York, NY 10032
Phone: (212) 543-5000

The Institute of Living (O, I, P, R)

400 Washington St.
Hartford, CT 06106
Phone: (860) 545-7200; (860) 545-7203; (800) 673-2411

The Laureate (I, P, R)

6655 S. Yale
Tulsa, OK 74136
Phone: (800) 322-5173; (918) 491-8106; (918) 298-7804

Linden Oaks Hospital (I, P, O)

852 West St.
Naperville, IL 60540-6400
Phone: (800) 955-OAKS or (630) 305-5500

The Meadows (I)

1655 No. Tegner St.
Wickenburg, AZ 85390
Phone: (800) MEADOWS; (520) 684-3926; (520) 684-3935

Medical University of South Carolina, Institute of Psychiatry
(I, P, O)

171 Ashley Ave.
Charleston, SC 29425-0742
Phone: (803) 792-0092

The Menninger Clinic (I, P, R)

Box 829
Topeka, KS 66601-0829
Phone: (913) 273-7500, ext. 5311; (800) 351-9058

Montecatini (R)

2516 La Costa Ave.
Rancho La Costa, CA 92009
Phone: (619) 436-8930

Monte Nido Residential Treatment Facility (R)
27162 Sea Vista Dr.
Malibu, CA 90265
Phone: (818) 222-9534

The New York Hospital–Cornell Medical Center (O)
525 East 68th St.
New York, NY 10021
Phone: (212) 746-3800

**The New York Hospital–Cornell Medical Center,
Westchester Division** (O, I, R)
21 Bloomingdale Rd.
White Plains, NY 10605
Phone: (914) 997-4310

The Rader Institute (I, P)
Corporate Office:
1663 Sawtelle Blvd.
Los Angeles, CA 90025
Phone: (800) 255-1818
(Several locations around the country)

Remuda Ranch Arizona (R)
Box 2481 Jack Burden Rd.
Wickenburg, AZ 85358
Phone: (800) 445-1900; (602) 684-3913

Renfrew Center (P, R)
475 Spring Lane
Philadelphia, PA 19128
Phone: (800) 736-3739

alternate location:
7700 Renfrew Lane
Coconut Creek, FL 33073
Phone: (800) 332-8415

Ridgeview Institute (I)
3995 So. Cobb Dr.
Smyrna, GA 30080
Phone: (800) 329-9775, ext. 4114

River Oaks, New Orleans (I, P, R)

1525 River Oaks Rd. West
New Orleans, LA 70123
Phone: (800) 366-1740; (504) 734-1740; fax: (504) 733-7020

Timberlawn Mental Health System (O)

4600 Samuell Blvd.
Dallas, TX 75228
Phone: (214) 381-7181

UCLA Neuro Psychiatric Institute (I, P)

UCLA, A South
405 Hilgard Ave.
Los Angeles,CA 90095
Phone: (310) 794-2093

University of Iowa Hospitals and Clinics (I, P)

UIHC
200 Hawkins Dr., 2887 JPP
Iowa City, IA 52242
Phone: (319) 356-1354; (319) 353-6149

University of Kansas School of Medicine, Wichita (I, O)

8901 East Orme
Wichita, KS 67207
Phone: (800) 322-8901; (316) 686-5000

University of Minnesota Hospital Eating Disorder Program
(I, P, O)

Box 393 Mayo
University of Minnesota Hospital
Minneapolis, MN 55455
Phone: (612) 626-6871

Western Psychiatric Institute and Clinic (I, P, O)

University of Pittsburgh Medical Center
Center for Overcoming Problem Eating (COPE)
3811 O'Hara St.
Pittsburgh, PA 15213
Phone: (412) 624-3507; (412) 624-0227

The Willough at Naples, Florida (I, P)
9001 Tamiami Trail East
Naples, FL 34113
Phone: (800) 722-0100; (813) 775-4500

Bibliography

Abernathy, R. P., and D. R. Black. "Healthy Body Weights: An Alternative Perspective." *American Journal of Clinical Nutrition* 63 (1996) (suppl.):448S.

Abraham, Suzanne, and Derek Llewellyn-Jones. *Eating Disorders: The Facts.* New York: Oxford University Press, 1992.

American Psychiatric Association. *Diagnostic and Statistical Manual of Mental Disorders,* 4th ed. Washington, D.C., 1994.

"Binge-Eating That Plagues Adults Now Recognized as a Disorder." *Environmental Nutrition Newsletter.* 20(8):1,6, Aug. 1997.

Bosello, O., et al. "Adipose Tissue Cellularity and Weight Reduction Forecasting." *American Journal of Clinical Nutrition* 33 (1980): 776–82.

"Breaking The Drinking Habit," *Psychology Today.* March–April 1995, p. 12.

Brewerton, T. D., and B. S. Dansky, "The National Women's Study: Prevalence of Criminal Victimization and PTSD in Bulimia Nervosa and Binge Eating Disorder." *Abstract Book: Annual Meeting of the National Eating Disorders Organization.* Columbus, Ohio, Oct. 1993.

Bruch, Hilde. *The Golden Cage: The Enigma of Anorexia Nervosa.* New York: Random House, 1978.

Chernin, Kim. *The Obsession: Reflections on the Tyranny of Slenderness.* New York: Harper & Row, 1981.

Coleman, Ray. *The Carpenters: The Untold Story—An Authorized Biography.* New York: HarperCollins, 1994.

Cooper, Peter J. *Bulimia Nervosa and Binge-Eating: A Guide to Recovery.* New York: New York University Press, 1996.

Copel, Linda Carman. *Nurse's Clinical Guide: Psychiatric and Mental Health Care.* Springhouse, Pa.: Springhouse Corp., 1996.

Costin, Carolyn. *The Eating Disorder Sourcebook.* Los Angeles: Lowell House, 1996.

deZwaan, M., and Mitchell, J. E. "Binge Eating in the Obese." *Annals of Medicine* 24 (1992): 303–308.

Dobie, Michael. "A Triple Threat." *Los Angeles Times,* 9/8/97, p. S6.

Enright, A. B., P. Butterfield, and B. Berkowitz. "Self-help and Support Groups in the Management of Eating Disorders." *Handbook of Psychotherapy for Anorexia Nervosa and Bulimia,* ed. D. M. Garner and P. Garfinkel. New York: Guilford Press, 1985.

Enright, Amy Baker, and Collen Tootell. "The Role of Support Groups in the Treatment of Eating Disorders." *American Mental Health Counselors Association Journal* (Oct. 1986): 237–45.

Ewen, Stuart. *All Consuming Images: The Politics of Style in Contemporary Culture.* New York: Basic Books, 1988.

Fairburn, Christopher. *Overcoming Binge Eating.* New York: The Guilford Press, 1995.

Fraser, Laura. *Losing It: America's Obsession with Weight and the Industry That Feeds On It.* New York: Dutton, 1997.

Gainsley, Bruce. "Treatment of Anorexia with Prozac." *Journal of Clinical Psychiatry* 51(Sept. 1990):378–82.

Garchik, Leah. Personals. *San Francisco Chronicle,* Dec. 9, 1993.

Garfinkel, P. E. "Perception of Hunger and Satiety in Anorexia Nervosa." *Psychological Medicine* 4(1974):309–15.

Garner, D. M., and P. E. Garfinkel. "Socio-cultural Factors in the Development of Anorexia Nervosa." *Psychological Medicine* 10(1980):647–56.

Gortmaker, Steven. "Social and Economic Consequences of Overweight in Adolescence and Young Adulthood." *Journal of the American Medical Association* 266(1993): 1008–12.

Gray, J. J. and K. Ford. "The Incidence of Bulimia in a College Sample." *International Journal of Eating Disorders* 4(1985):201–21.

Haskew, Paul, and Cynthia H. Adams. *Eating Disorders: Managing Problems with Food.* Mission Hills, Calif.: Glencoe, 1989.

Hesse-Biber, Sharlene. *Am I Thin Enough Yet? The Cult of*

Thinness and the Commercialization of Identity. New York: Oxford University Press, 1996.

Hittner, Patricia. "Dying to Be Thin." *Better Homes and Gardens* 75(8)(Aug. 1997): 84–88.

Holland, A. J., et al. "Anorexia Nervosa: Study of 34 Twin Pairs and 1 Set of Triplets." *British Journal of Psychiatry* 145(1984):414–19.

Johnson, C., C. Lewis, and J. Hagman. "The Syndrome of Bulimia: Review and Synthesis." *The Psychiatric Clinics of North America* 7(1984):247–73.

Kessler, M. and G. W. Albee. "Primary Prevention." *Annual Review of Psychology* 26(1975):557–91.

Keys, A., et al. *The Biology of Human Starvation.* Minneapolis, Minn.: University of Minnesota Press, 1950.

Kirkland, Gelsey, and Greg Lawrence. *Dancing on My Grave.* Garden City, N.Y.: Doubleday & Co., 1986.

Kluft, R., ed. *Incest-Related Syndromes of Adult Psychopathology.* Washington, D.C.: American Psychiatric Association Press, 1990.

Kog, E., R. Pierloot, and W. Vandereycken. "Methodological Considerations of Family Research in Anorexia Nervosa." *International Journal of Eating Disorders* 2 (4)(1983):79–83.

Kratina, Karin. "10 Things Coaches Can Do to Help Prevent Eating Disorders in Their Athletes." *National Eating Disorders Organization Newsletter* XXX(1)(Spring 1996):6.

Levine, Michael. "Basic Ingredients of a Good Program for the Treatment and Management of Eating Disorders." Presented at the 13th National NEDO Conference, Columbus, Ohio, Oct. 3, 1994.

Levine, Michael. "Summary of Findings Concerning Weight and Shape Concerns in Late Childhood and Adolescence." Presented at the 13th National NEDO Conference, Columbus, Ohio, Oct. 3, 1994.

Maine, Margo. "What Men Need to Know About Eating Disorders." Handout from Eating Disorders Awareness & Prevention, Inc., Seattle, Wash. 1994, 1–3.

Mehren, Elizabeth, and Michael J. Ybarra. "A Dancer's Death Hints at 'A Cult of Secrecy.' " *Los Angeles Times,* July 17, 1997, Section E, p. 1.

Minuchin, S., B. L. Rosman, and L. Baker. *Psychosomatic Families: Anorexia Nervosa in Context.* Cambridge, Mass.: Harvard University Press, 1978.

Morton, Andrew. *Diana: Her True Story.* New York: Pocket Books, 1992.

O'Neill, Cherry Boone. *Starving for Attention.* Minneapolis, Minn.: LifeCare Books, 1992.

Oppenheimer et al. "Adverse Sexual Experiences in Childhood and Clinical Eating Disorders: A Preliminary Description." *Journal of Psychiatric Research* 19(1985):157–61.

Pena, Ellen Hart. "Hitting Her Stride: A Runner Goes the Distance, Beating Anorexia and Bulimia." *People,* Apr. 10, 1995, pp. 115–120.

Pipher, Mary. *Reviving Ophelia: Saving the Selves of Adolescent Girls.* New York: Ballantine Books, 1995.

Ponton, Lynn E. "A Review of Eating Disorders in Adolescents." *Adolescent Psychiatry: Developmental and Clinical Studies, Vol. 20,* ed. Richard C. Marohn and Sherman C. Feinstein. Hillsdale, N.J.: Analytic Press, 1995.

Pope, H. G., et al. "Childhood Sexual Abuse and Bulimia Nervosa: A Comparison of American, Austrian and Brazilian Women." *American Journal of Psychiatry* 151(1994):732, 737.

Reiff, D. W. and K. K. Reiff. *Eating Disorders: Nutrition Therapy in the Recovery Process.* Aspen, Md.: Aspen Publishers 1992.

Robinson, P. H. "The Bulimic Disorders." *Clinical Neuropharmacology* 9(1)(1986):14–36.

Rosen, Lionel W., et al. "Pathogenic Weight-Control Behavior in Female Athletes." *The Physician and Sportsmedicine* 14(1) (1986).

Rosen, M., et al. "Eating Disorders: A Hollywood History." *People,* Feb. 17, 1992, 96–98.

Sandbek, Terence J. *The Deadly Diet,* 2nd ed. Oakland, Calif.: New Harbinger Publications, Inc., 1993.

Sanz, Cynthia. "Happy As They Are." *People,* Sept. 29, 1997, p. 48.

Satter, Ellyn. *Child of Mine: Feeding with Love and Good Sense.* Palo Alto, Calif.: Bull Publishing Co., 1986.

Schneider, Karen S., et al. "Mission Impossible." *People,* June 3, 1996, p. 71.

Seligmann, Jean, Patrick Rogers, and Peter Annin. "The Pressure to Lose." *Newsweek,* May 2, 1994, pp. 60–61.

Siegel, Michele, Judith Brisman, and Margot Weinshel. *Surviving an Eating Disorder: Strategies for Family and Friends—Revised and Updated.* New York: HarperCollins, 1997.

"Special Report: Eating Disorders." *Sports Illustrated.* August 8, 1994, pp. 54–60.

Sporkin, Elizabeth, Joyce Wagner, and Craig Tomashoff. "A Terrible Hunger." *People,* February 17, 1992, pp. 92–95.

Sundgot-Borgen, J. "Prevalence of Eating Disorders in Elite Female Athletes." *International Journal of Sports Nutrition* 3(1)(1993):29–40.

Tiggemann, M., and E. E. Rothblum. "Gender Differences in Social Consequences of Perceived Overweight in the United States and Australia." *Sex Roles* 18(1988):75–86.

Tribole, Evelyn and Resch, Elyse. *Intuitive Eating.* New York: St. Martin's Press, 1995.

Walsh, T., et. al. "Medication and Psychotherapy in the Treatment of Bulimia Nervosa." *American Journal of Psychiatry* 154(4)(Apr. 1997): 523–31.

Warren, B. J., A. L. Stanton, and D. L. Blessing. "Disordered Eating Patterns in Competitive Female Athletes." *International Journal of Eating Disorders* 9(5)(1990): 565–69.

Woo, Lynne M. H. "Diet Counseling: Treatment of Anorexia Nervosa and Bulimia." *Topics in Clinical Nutrition* 1(1)(1986): 73–84.

Yager, J. "The Treatment of Eating Disorders." *Journal of Clinical Psychiatry* 49 (suppl.) (1988): 18–25.

Yager, J. "The Treatment of Bulimia: An Overview." *Current Treatment of Anorexia Nervosa and Bulimia,* ed. P. S. Powers and R. C. Fernandez. Basel, Switzerland: Karger, 1984.

Yates, A. "Current Perspectives on the Eating Disorders: I. History, Psychological, and Biological Aspects." *Journal of American Academy of Child and Adolescent Psychiatry* 28(1989):813–28.

Endnotes

Chapter 1

[1]Although the incidence of eating disorders among males has increased in recent years, 90 percent of the sufferers are female. In the interest of simplicity, we will refer to those with eating disorders as "she," although most of the information also applies to men.

[2]Kirkland, p. 104.

[3]Coleman, p. 312.

[4]The National Association of Anorexia Nervosa and Associated Disorders.

[5]This is *not* the same as generalized overeating (or grazing) or occasional episodes of overeating (e.g., during a party or when experiencing a stressful event). Binge eating is episodic and includes a huge number of calories. Eating two pieces of cake and feeling guilty afterward does not constitute a binge.

[6]Costin, p. 30.

[7]Costin, pp. 20–21.

[8]Boone, p. 95.

[9]Fairburn.

[10]American Psychiatric Association, *DSM-IV.*

[11]The method of determining frequency is different for binge eating disorder than for bulimia nervosa. Currently binge eating is counted in days, while bulimia is counted in episodes. Therefore, five episodes of binge eating in one day would be counted as only one, while five episodes of bingeing/purging would be counted as five. Further research is needed to determine whether binge eating should be counted per episode when diagnosing the condition.

[12]The National Association of Anorexia Nervosa and Associated Disorders.

[13]American Psychiatric Association.

[14]Fairburn, deZwaan, M., and Mitchell, J. E., p. 303.

[15]Gray and Ford, p. 201.

[16]Rosen, L.W., et al.

[17]Costin, p. 21.

Chapter 2

[1]Fraser, p. 43.
[2]Pena, p. 119.
[3]Abernathy and Black, p. 448.
[4]Haskew and Adams, pp. 53–54.
[5]Bosello, et al., p. 776
[6]Fraser, p. 8.
[7]Ibid.
[8]Ewen, p. 179.
[9]Fraser, p. 39.
[10]Schneider, p. 71.
[11]Ibid.
[12]Ibid.
[13]Abraham and Llewellyn-Jones, p. 9.
[14]Quoted in "Slim Chances," *Los Angeles Times*, 7/31/90.

Chapter 3

[1]Warren, Stanton, and Blessing, p. 566.
[2]Rosen, L. W., et al.
[3]Rosen, M., et al., p. 97.
[4]Ibid.
[5]Ibid.
[6]Garner and Garfinkel, p. 649.
[7]Oppenheimer et al., p. 159.
[8]Ibid.
[9]Seligmann, Rogers, and Annin, p. 61.
[10]American Psychiatric Association, *DSM-IV*.
[11]Seligmann, Rogers and Annin, p. 60.

Chapter 4

[1]Haskew and Adams, p. 98.
[2]Keys et al., p. 837.
[3]Cooper, p. 34.
[4]Sandbek, p. 37.
[5]Ibid.

Chapter 6

[1]Sporkin, Wagner, and Tomashoff, p. 93.
[2]Coleman, p. 325.
[3]Siegel, Brisman, and Weinshel, pp. 92–110.
[4]Morton, pp. 147–148.
[5]O'Neill, pp. 175–178.
[6]Costin, p. 85.

Chapter 7

[1]Satter, p. 409.
[2]Developed by dietitians and nutritionists who are advocates of size acceptance; their efforts are coordinated by Joanne P. Ikeda, M.A., R.D., Nutrition Education Specialist, Dept. of Nutritional Services, University of California, Berkeley, CA 94720-3104.
[3]Adapted from Maine, M. pp. 1–3.
[4]Sundgot-Borgen, p. 31.
[5]Dobie, p. 56.
[6]Kratina, p. 6.

Chapter 8

[1]Rosen, M., et al., p. 97.
[2]Ibid.
[3]Tribole and Resch, p. 240.

Index